# TRUE
# TO
# TYPE

# TRUE
# TO
# TYPE

## Answers to the Most Commonly Asked Questions About Interpreting The Myers-Briggs Type Indicator

William C. Jeffries

HAMPTONROADS
PUBLISHING COMPANY, INC.

MBTI and the Myers-Briggs Type Indicator are registered trademarks of Consulting Psychologists Press, Palo Alto, California.

Type-o-graphics are a trademark of FarCreations. Diagrams and concepts are used with their permission.

For information write:

Hampton Roads Publishing Company, Inc.
891 Norfolk Square
Norfolk, VA 23502

Or call: (804)459-2453
   (FAX: (804)455-8907

If you are unable to order this book from your local bookseller, you may order directly from the publisher. Quantity discounts for organizations are available. Call 1-800-766-8009, toll-free.

ISBN 1-878901-08-7

10 9 8 7 6

Printed in the United States of America

# ACKNOWLEDGEMENTS

Anyone writing today about the MBTI or psychological type has a host of predecessors whose collective wisdom has informed their ideas. I am particularly thankful to Katharine C. Briggs and Isabel Briggs Myers for bringing the theory of type to life and to Dr. Mary H. McCaulley for having done so much in her lifetime to perpetuate the authors' ideas and to work to help establish the intellectual and professional credibility of the theory through her research.

I also owe a special debt of gratitude to several people who have read my manuscript and contributed suggestions, ideas, and anecdotes. Others have offered me encouragement to pursue this project as a necessary contribution to our ongoing understanding of psychological type and its ethical use. Dr. Leonard D. Goodstein and Judith Noel in particular have helped me to refine both ideas and methods of presentation. Otto Kroeger was an early mentor and ignited my interest in psychological type. I am also indebted to Frank DeMarco for his careful reading of my text before its publication. To these and countless others, mostly colleagues, friends, clients, and students with whom I have worked, I say: Thank-you.

William C. Jeffries, INTJ
Virginia Beach, Virginia

for my children,
Tiffany, Ainsley, and Joshua,
who every day remind me of the beauty,
power, and richness of diversity in our lives.

Thank you

# TABLE OF CONTENTS

# INDEX TO QUESTIONS

35. I know that you have said that there are no good types and no bad types, but, honestly, don't "P's" procrastinate more than "J's"?

36. As an ENFP, why do I have such a hard time introducing myself to others or sharing personal insights during presentations? Aren't I supposed to be gregarious and friendly?

37. I hear people talk about "working out of their shadow function." What does that mean?

38. How often should I take the MBTI?

39. Can't I come out any type I want to on the MBTI?

40. Is any one of my four letters more important or more influential than the others?

41. Can I use the MBTI to hire the right employee for a job?

42. Should I use my type to choose a career?

43. Does being an "F" mean that I am more emotional than my "T" associates?

44. Sixteen letters are a lot to remember. Do you have any tips for remembering what all these letters mean?

45. How am I likely to act in regard to my type when I am under stress?

46. I have seen some recent criticism of the MBTI that suggests that it is little more than a quaint parlor game because all it indicates is positive traits about a person. What do you say?

47. Is there an ideal sequence of events when presenting a feedback session to a group of people?

48. You have discussed a great number of the benefits one derives from taking the MBTI, but what is the downside? What possible negative consequences can occur when organizations use the MBTI?

49. Is there any significance to the order in which the letters in the type formula appear?

50. How can I best describe the MBTI and the associated preferences to an audience? What, exactly, should I use as examples?

# PREFACE:

# OK, I'VE GOT A QUESTION

As I travel from organization to organization, I hear the same questions being raised, often from people who have heard presentations on the MBTI several times. Some of these questions come from individuals who have already attended week-long workshops designed to provide participants with the adequate skills to be recommended as qualified users of the indicator. I could posit hundreds of questions and offer answers based on the Manual (see Bibliography under Myers for this definitive work on the MBTI), other MBTI literature, and my own experience, but instead I have decided to limit the questions to just those I have heard frequently. The arbitrary criterion I have chosen to admit a question to this list is that I must have been asked the same question at least five times over the last year. I can't guarantee that I have given the same answer each time, but these are the answers I have worked toward during my years of presenting the MBTI to audiences around the world.

Since I, as you, continue to grow in my knowledge of type, I would be delighted to talk to you if you believe any of my answers miss the mark or if you would simply like to refine, expand, or chat about any of my comments. Even if you would just like to say "Hi!" you can contact me at:

Executive Strategies International
(800) 594-4867

In answering the following questions, I have tried to give succinct, correct responses. I do not intend that the answer is, at all times, complete. Some of the questions, quite obviously, have been the subject of entire books by other authors. I have endeavored not to repeat what others have already said. Although my answers may be brief, I have tried to avoid glib or superficial responses. In most cases, I have avoided the cant of psychometricians in favor of more colloquial speech. The risk I run is that I will not sound scholarly in my answers. For that violation of decorum, I'll ask your forgiveness in advance. What I hope I put forward is an answer that will work for you if you are ever called to task. Some of my answers are based on research, some on experience, and some on conjecture. I will do my best to be clear in each case which it is. If I can cite any other authority to help clarify my answers, I will.

If you are relatively new to type, I suggest you start at the end of the book with the section called "What It Is and What it Isn't." This section will ground you in the basics of the MBTI or provide you a practical review of what the eight choices actually mean.

# TRUE
# TO
# TYPE

# 50 QUESTIONS

## QUESTION 1: Where do our preferences come from?

This is a question frequently asked in virtually every session, particularly if the consultant fails to deal with it during the formal presentation. Schools of developmental psychology fall into camps with one of two operating premises: nature or nurture. Those who hold to the former see genetics as the factor responsible for human characteristics. Those who hold to the latter see environment as the factor responsible. Those who hold to the validity of type theory are found in each camp. That distinction is complicated by the fact that Jungians can also be found in either camp. As I read Jung, however, it becomes clear that Jung himself ascribed our traits to genetics. In other words, according to Jung, we are born with our preferences. But while type theory begins with Jung, there is not a perfect congruence. Clearly, our preferences are also shaped, molded, reinforced, or restricted by our environment: friends, family, religious training, jobs, etc. Type, then, for me is a reflection of both nature and nurture. Both play a role in who we see ourselves to be and what we prefer.

## QUESTION 2: I've heard some people talk about "True Type." How does that differ from my "Myers-Briggs Type"?

The distinction being raised is an important one to be made in any presentation. In short, the four letters a client receives may or may not be the person's "true type." The client must be the one to make that decision. The theory holds that each of us has a "true type." Whether or not the MBTI reflects that type at any one taking is, to a certain extent, up for grabs, depending on the circumstances, frame of mind, and "honesty" of the person taking the indicator.

There are several reasons why individuals may misreport themselves. Perhaps they find themselves in jobs where a certain style of behavior is expected and maybe even rewarded. Perhaps they have heard just enough about the MBTI from others to believe that a certain type is "better" for a job than others. For example, I once taught a graduate education class for about thirty teachers, all of whom were aspiring candidates for jobs as guidance counselors. As part of the program they all completed the MBTI. One of the individuals obtained access to a set of scoring keys and scored her answer sheet herself and discovered she had picked INTP. Having heard, somewhere, that the typical type for high school guidance directors was ESFJ, she went back and redid her answers, erasing almost every one, so that she would come out ESFJ when I tallied her responses. A simple, but not infrequent, misunderstanding of how the results might be used had caused this problem.

I have also had an army general officer provide some real insights as to how strongly we can be scripted by our jobs and colleagues. This person had taken the MBTI four times during his career. The first three times he had elected ISTJ (the modal type, by the way, for the armed forces). When I met him he had just received his results for the fourth time. This time he scored INTP. After we had talked for some time, he admitted, "It has taken me a long time to get here, but finally I've had enough confidence in my abilities to report myself as I truly see my preferences." He went on to say that he knew then that he had been masquerading for years as an ISTJ in behavior, because that kind of behavior won applause from his community. That behavior—that mask, to use Jungian terms—had been reflected in his responses each previous occasion. Unfortunately, the act, for many years, had become the person. Sad to say, that same dilemma faces many people in many professions. We often hear subtly or more overtly, "shape up or ship out!"

Family pressures to conform can likewise discourage individuals from reporting honest "preferences" on the indicator. Our research has shown, for example, a disproportionate number (as would be expected in the general population) of INFP children in military families, where the predominant uniformed parent is ISTJ and the other parent is ISFJ. Is the reported type an indication of rebellion, the desire to provide something different from what they see as the norm, the need for flexibility in an otherwise rigid system, the need to be able to respond to frequent moves, or "true type?" We just don't know. The individual is the final arbiter. In families of corporate executives where the spousal types are much the same as above, we see much the same kind of data, although the sample size is much more suspect.

Of course there are other reasons as well that individuals may misreport their types. These reasons range from being under stress to misunderstanding the questions or the words. There are also those who may have been culturally, socially, or linguistically disadvantaged and those whose level of education is inadequate to respond to the questions. Those for whom English is a second language, those from non-white, non-male groups, or those people just enjoying normal developmental changes may likewise misreport themselves. The burden is on the consultant, however, to ensure that clients do not assume that the indicator is telling them their type. Each individual must decide for himself or herself. The language we should use in reporting a person's type, therefore, should be something like:

"When you took the indicator you reported yourself as ____"

## QUESTION 3: How reliable are my results?

Usually when people ask this question they asking whether or not they can trust their results to reflect their true personalities and behaviors. They are not, in other words, really asking about "reliability." So it is best to press them about what they are really asking. If they want to know to what extent the indicator really measures those things it claims to measure, they are concerned with **validity**, or the degree to which inferences about the results can be supported by evidence. Psychometricians traditionally discuss validity in terms of criterion-related, content-related, and construct-related forms of evidence. Most users of the indicator need not worry about such fine distinctions because the validation has already been done for them. Chapter 11 of the Manual provides solid documentation of the indicator's high validity. From time to time, however, the language surfaces in questions, and knowledgeable users will want to be able to respond appropriately.

If those asking the questions truly understand what **reliability** means, then you must answer a different question. Chances are they are asking what the likelihood is that they will replicate their results on retake—in short, they are asking about take-retake reliability. In that case, chapter 10 of the Manual is your source. The reliability of the results depends on several things (gender, age, education, achievement level, and all those issues discussed in Question 2). It also depends on the strength of the individual preferences—the clearer the preference, the higher the reliability. The consensus is that a personality indicator should be 70% or higher to be considered reliable. Taking all things into consideration, one can see that the MBTI is about 85% reliable—that's impressively high reliability. To be any more specific in positing differing reliabilities according to preference strengths, as some trainers do, is to stretch the data beyond its elasticity.

Some trainers routinely refer to subscores or subscales when interpreting MBTI results (see Question 18). These individuals, to be responsible, incur special responsibilities. Proper standards for psychological testing suggest that when subscores are reported, it is not sufficient to report reliabilities solely for overall scores but that reliabilities should also be reported for any subscores that are discussed. Chapter 10, again, is the source for this valuable information.

## QUESTION 4: If my colleague and I are the same type, why are we so different?

With this question, the client has hit on one of the exciting attributes of the MBTI. Type does not constrict us or demand that we perform in prescribed ways. While a knowledge of type can give us an understanding of predictable differences in individuals and, therefore, allow us to deal with those differences in a more constructive way, it in no way determines our behavior. It simply helps us to see "that much seemingly chance variation in human behavior is not due to chance; it is in fact the logical result of a few basic, observable preferences." (Manual, P. 11).

Once you know that Bill Jeffries is an INTJ, you do not know precisely how I will act at any given time. What you do know is that when my personality was in the process of forming, I picked Yankee Stadium, not Shea Stadium. But once I'm in the ballpark, there are about 50,000 seats for me to move among. Far from boxing us in, type theory gives us a chance to deal with diversity in the workplace in a much more productive way, truly cherishing our differences for the strengths they bring. Each person is unique, despite his or her preferences.

Having participants with the same preferences meet and discuss their preferences with one another can be a very informative process. Of course they are going to feel at home together; there will be similar ways of dealing with the world. Often, however, the insights they gain are around differences—sometimes slight, sometimes substantial. Such a process helps individuals understand the nonrestrictive nature of their preferences.

Furthermore, there may be differences between colleagues of the same psychological type for reasons for which type offers no answer. No paper and pen indicator, however well conceived and normed, can sum up human personality. Those of us who appreciate so much the work that Katharine Briggs and Isabel Briggs Myers did to bring the indicator into being, sometimes have a hard time admitting this fact, but type doesn't explain everything. Human personality is far too rich. If personality were to be illustrated by an iceberg, then perhaps type is the rather substantial tip. But there is much more below the surface than there is above.

Type development and clarity of a person's preferences also play important roles in explaining why two people of the same type may be very different in behavior or appearance. I believe it was Isabel who said something like, "Every ESTJ is like **every** other ESTJ, like **some** other ESTJ's, and like **no** other ESTJ you may ever have met." Even if the story is apocryphal, the sentiment is true. An INFP with preference strengths of I-1, N-3, F-5, & P-3 is behaviorally a very different person than an INFP with preference strengths of 55, 49, 31, & 59. In fact, a person with very clear INFP preferences may well experience an INFP colleague with less clear preferences as an "E," "S," "T," or "J." What we observe as preferences is often a matter of degree. This is partially the reason why it is often difficult to guess the type of a loved one. We see that person in comparison to ourselves.

Similarly, if a person has achieved some degree of good type development (see Question 22), he or she has learned when to use the appropriate preference, whether favored or not. For instance, as a golfer, I may prefer using my driver over the other clubs. But even though it is my preferred club, I'm a stupid golfer if I try to putt with it. It's just an analogy to be sure, but it is an apt analogy to type. What I want, if I'm a well developed golfer, is a bag of clubs from which I can choose depending on the shot. Making that choice does not naysay the fact that I have a favorite; sometimes, to be pragmatic, I must use a non-preferred club. When individuals have achieved some level of good type development, they occasionally use their non-preferences with some skill. Their behavior at these times may be seen by others as running counter to type.

## QUESTION 5: Can I change my type?

The theory says there is a true type for each individual. If the client is asking about this type, then the answer is **no.** If the client means can the reported type change, see Question 2. Often what this question is attempting to probe, however, is the differences in themselves that people see as they mature. Clearly, we do change, we do develop as we go through life, but those changes are more a reflection of our types than they are changes in our types. The theory says we have a type, and if we have accurately identified that type, it does not change.

## QUESTION 6: I am a very different person at home from the person I am on the job. How does your theory and data explain that?

This is a common observation that often arises. Sometimes the question is raised because the individual has not received the proper directions for filling out the MBTI. The frame of reference an individual uses to answer the questions can color some responses. Unfortunately the directions on the back of the answer sheet are not as clear as they could be. The point to keep in mind is that the MBTI is a preference indicator based on theory, not behavior. Yet the directions say: "Read one question at a time, with both (or all) its answers, and choose the way you more often feel or act" (Myers-Briggs Type Indicator Form G, answer sheet). The directions seem to tell the respondent to answer behaviorally.

I prefer to be clearer about the purpose and suggest that the client answer all questions with the frame of reference, "Given the best of all possible worlds, what would you prefer to do, how would you prefer to act, which word appeals more to you?" With this frame of reference, then, the client has a greater chance of registering the same preferences, regardless of the setting.

But there are some other interesting offshoots from this question. Sometimes, sitting in the office filling out the MBTI, a client may register a set of preferences that differs from the preferences he or she registers when filling out the MBTI while sitting at home. The client will say, "See, I really am a different person at home from the one I am at work. At work I'm hard-chargin', bottom-line-oriented, and maybe a little rigid. But you have to be; that's the nature of the job. But at home, I'm a kinder and gentler person, more open to feedback and the concerns of my family."

Well, as in any business, the customer may be right. But more often than not, people who report their type one way on the job and another way at home are just fooling themselves. When I give the MBTI to the spouse to fill out on how he or she sees the spouse at home, the report is routinely the same as the one on the job. In other words, we are very successful in lying to ourselves in thinking that we have dropped a lot more at the office than we have. The family simply does not see us the way we think we are behaving. That misconception can be crucial information for us to know.

## QUESTION 7: Is type related to horoscope?

Depending on the client's perspective regarding astrology you could have good news or bad news. The informal comparisons that people tell me they have done—none very rigorous—point to there being no correlation between a person's horoscope and type. There are some interesting similarities and some intriguing relationships but no correlations. Perhaps the reason this question is raised so frequently is the way type is often reported to the client. Invariably some set of personality portraits is given out with the report form. Because of the nature of type (with our overlapping preferences) we can often find something about ourselves in almost any of the sixteen types. Likewise, persons scanning the horoscopes in the newspaper can find things under several of the signs that seem to correspond with their lives. The similarities seem keen, but the limited research done does not justify the relationship.

# QUESTION 8: Why do we have to pick between just two answers, (A) or (B)?

On 117 of the 126 questions on Form G of the MBTI, one does have to choose between just (A) or (B). For eight of the questions there is also a (C) choice, and for one question there is also a (D) alternative. While some types predictably find the A-B choices irritating, such a format merely reflects the dichotomous nature of Jung's theory. While all of us "E & I," "S & N," "T & F," and "J & P," we only do one at a time. In other words, before I begin to extravert, I have to stop introverting. Consequently, at any given time I can only do one or the other. Since each question on the indicator deals with only one function or attitude pair, while I may (A) and (B) at different times, I can only do one at a time; hence, I have to choose. A mathematical correlation of the sum total of the times you pick (A) or (B) will show your preferences.

Here's another explanation that often clarifies the dichotomous nature of the choices. When an artilleryman learns gunnery, he learns how to hit a target with a round by first bracketing the target. He fires a round to the left (call that "A") and a round to the right (call that "B"). Once he sees where the rounds land, he narrows the bracket and fires two more rounds. He continues to narrow the bracket until the rounds fall directly on top of the target. The command then is "fire for effect," and the rounds land right on target. Something akin to that is happening with the indicator. The client is asked to make 21 choices between "E" & "I," 26 choices between "S" & "N," 23 choices between "T" & "F," and 24 choices between "J" & "P." Once the client has indicated choices that many times (narrowed the bracket, if you will), the scorer can say "fire for effect." These are the four targets you have selected.

The other aspect of the choices that often irritates people is the expectation of certain types (usually those with a "T" in their type formula) that the choices be logically opposed. That, after all, has been the pattern established through years of test taking in school. The only problem is that the choices on the MBTI are not necessarily **logical** opposites; instead, they are often psychological opposites. The dichotomous nature of the choices, therefore, not only causes some interesting psychometric properties for the researcher (such as having bi-modal distributions for the four scales), but it also prompts some queries from clients.

## QUESTION 9: I couldn't answer some of the questions. Will my results still be usable?

The short answer is, probably yes. It all depends on the number of omissions and how they are distributed. Unfortunately some consultants tell their clients that they have to answer every question on the indicator. That was never the authors' intent. The instructions for taking the MBTI direct the client to answer as many questions as possible. If the client has no clear choice, however, he or she should leave the question unanswered. If the question of how many answers a client may leave blank comes up, the Manual provides the guidance that one can accept up to 25 random omissions on Form G and 35 on Form F and still maintain stable reliabilities. So, in my instructions to the client, I discourage but allow omissions. With many omissions, however, you should question the results.

## QUESTION 10: Why do many Jungians reject the J-P preference on the MBTI?

The Myers-Briggs Type Indicator was designed consciously to "make the theory of psychological types described by C. G. Jung understandable and useful in people's lives" (Manual, p. 1). To many Jungians, having the Judging-Perceiving attitude included on the MBTI represents a violation of Jungian theory. While the J-P difference was never explicitly stated in Jung's writings, Katharine and Isabel felt it was there implicitly. I, and others knowledgeable in the field, agree with their judgment, but many "pure" Jungians take umbrage at such liberties being taken with the theory. One way to overcome any misgivings regarding this distinction on the indicator is to divide your group into "J" and "P" groups and give them an assignment: plan a meeting; decide what to do with excess year-end funds; decide how a teacher should assign work for the day; or perform some similar exercise that will explore the difference between those who want to schedule and control and those who prefer to remain open to what occurs. As you process the results, ask participants if they see any differences. Often, the "J" - "P" dichotomy is one of the clearest to observe.

## QUESTION 11: Why do several questions seem to ask the same thing?

The issue is more than just "seeming." Many questions on the indicator do in fact attempt to elicit the same information (see Question 8 for specifics). By asking a series of seemingly inconsequential questions, the indicator attempts to elicit responses about eight preferences regarding human personality. The more questions one asks about the same preferences, the higher the potential reliability of the results. The various shadings of the questions attempt to flesh out different possible understandings of what the questions mean, in an attempt to have those taking the indicator render the clearest possible results.

Some types ( not unusually those with "N" and "T" preferences) will spot this feature of the indicator more quickly than others. Often, the temptation will be to try to be as consistent as possible in answering all the questions the same way, out of a concern that if they don't, such inconsistency might imply something negative or strange. Such conscious "gaming" ought to be discouraged. Simply ask the client to respond honestly to each question.

## QUESTION 12: Are intuitives more creative than sensors?

There are an unfortunately large number of consultants and creative thinking gurus who preach such a false gospel. NO, intuitives are not more creative than sensors. The two are simply creative in different ways. The language I prefer to use to describe the difference comes from research I have done with another indicator: the KAI — Kirton-Adaption-Innovation Inventory (an indicator designed by M. J. Kirton). This instrument, that measures one's style of creativity, posits the difference between generative creativity (an innovative style) and adaptive creativity. Not only because there are correlations between the two but also because the terms so aptly describe the process, I use the term Generative to describe the intuitive's style and the term Adaptive to describe the sensor's style. The specific exercise I use to demonstrate the difference is described in my book on psychological type and organizational applications. Indeed, much of the chapter on creativity is dedicated to "S"- "N" differences.

An intuitive, in being creative, is likely to scrap the entirety of what is currently being done. Whatever the current paradigm, it is up for grabs in the intuitive's search for a more creative way. If that paradigm is a system, a procedure, a set of rules, a tradition, or a customary way of doing things in an organization, then it should be clear why the intuitive is oftentimes seen as a little disruptive to the status quo. The intuitive is seen as not as "safe" as the more "stable" sensor who works within the system, the current paradigm, to accomplish change. By being more comfortable with what is and what has been, the sensor adapts his or her creativity to the existing framework and, therefore, can appear to be the better team player. But of course there is a tradeoff between the two styles:

**HIGH PAYOFF**

**low payoff +**

**SENSOR**                                                  **INTUITIVE**

_____

**low risk -**

**HIGH RISK**

What the payoff matrix attempts to highlight is that sensors' preferences can make them highly successful and effective working within existing organizational systems. They tend to capitalize on existing definitions and likely solutions. They are able to stretch the "givens" in new and creative ways. They focus on producing change using existing methods for improvement. But there is both good news and bad news about their style. The good news is that they are frequently successful in their efforts at change; the bad news is that the increment of success each time is likely to be relatively low.

Intuitives perceive quite differently! They tend to redefine the problem. They are often more concerned with doing something differently than with doing an established, standardized procedure better. Their solutions are less expected and in some cases less accepted. More innovative than adaptive, intuitives tend to go outside the established systems and methods for solutions. The good news is that when they are successful, the payoff can be very high. The bad news is that they tend to be successful at a much lower frequency than is the sensor. These differences in styles of creativity between sensors and intuitives, if not understood in terms of preferred style, can create havoc and interpersonal confusion within any organization.

Once managers become skilled in the recognition of these differences in individuals or organizations, they can be much more effective in accomplishing organizational objectives. Where the sensor's and intuitive's styles complement one another, we have a richer base for creativity. The sensor provides a safe base for the intuitive's riskier operations, and the intuitive provides the dynamics to bring about periodic radical change, without which institutions tend to ossify.

Neither sensors nor intuitives are more creative than the others.

## QUESTION 13: What do very high scores or very low scores indicate about a person? Which is better?

The short answer is that neither high nor low scores are necessarily good or bad. Unlike basketball, high score does not win, and unlike golf, low score does not win. There are, however, tradeoffs with each. First of all, the words high and low are red flags to many people. We unfortunately associate "high" with good and "low" with bad. The association probably stems back to concern with grades in school. Regretfully, the report forms used by most people to communicate preference strengths to clients also perpetuate this unconscious association.

In an effort to reflect faithfully the dichotomous nature of the theory and the scores, they are routinely sketched on a horizontal continuum with zero in the middle and the extremes to the left and the right. The scores for "E," "S," "T," & "J" are reported to the left of center, and the scores for "I," "N," "F," & "P" are reported to the right of center. Unfortunately we also learned in school that negative numbers are to the left and positive numbers are to the right. While this is a subtle influence to be sure, it may, nevertheless, be at work in a client's mind.

Rather than use the words high and low to describe preference strengths, I prefer the terms from the Manual: **Slight, Moderate, Clear, and Very Clear**. These terms connote less regarding relative desirability than do "high" or "low," or "strong" or "weak."

There are both good points and bad points associated with **very clear** preferences (41 or higher; 31 for "F"). What is known is only that the individual has a definite preference for that function or attitude. It may well be that the individual also has more ability with that preference because it is used more—much like a muscle that gets stronger by frequent exercise—but we do not know that. What we know is that persons with very clear preferences know their preferences, and by extrapolation, perhaps they know themselves better. The bad news is that when called upon to use the opposite preference, a person with such clarity of preferences often finds it more difficult to do the opposite.

The person with **slight** preferences (1-9) faces a somewhat different set of circumstances. On the plus side of the ledger, such a person may have greater ease in moving from one end of the spectrum to the other; perhaps that person can do both with some ease even though he or she still has a preference. The bad news is that such persons may themselves not know when they will do one or the other. Such a dilemma can cause confusion for the person and may well send mixed signals to others on the job.

Let's say a colleague has a "J" preference strength of 3. On Monday, someone sees him and asks for a decision. "Do it, " he says. "It sounds like a feasible course of action." On Tuesday, you present him with three courses of action. He says, "Implement number two." On Wednesday, I come in with a report I have been working on. It needs his approval before the report can go forward to the CFO. "Oh," he says, "let's hold off on sending this until we gather some more data on the soil samples at the Monroe plant." That comment—just born from his desire to play "P" for the day—runs the risk of telling me that I have blundered, I've missed the boat on the report, I failed to get the pertinent data.

While neither very clear nor slight preferences are necessarily good or bad, it is apparent from Jung's writings that he thought that persons ought to be clear about their preferences. A person with a slight strength can know his or her preference, and just understand that it is not very demonstrative. But Jung would warn that a person with slight preferences runs the risk of never truly developing them, and that would keep all preferences relatively underdeveloped—what he referred to as a "primitive mentality."

The important point to underscore, however, with anyone who has taken the indicator is that **"strength does not imply excellence"** (Manual, p. 58). The fact that I score I-37, N-51, T-29, and J-45, does not mean that I necessarily do any of them well; it just indicates that I have clear or very clear preferences throughout.

Preference strengths do not measure maturity, skill, ability, or development—simply preference.

## QUESTION 14: I thought balance was an important issue in psychological type. Now you seem to be saying that balance between preferences is not desirable. Please explain.

There is a crucial distinction to be made between balance between preferences and Balance as understood in Jungian theory. Balance as implied in this question would suggest relative equality of "E & I," "S & N," "T & F," or "J & P." In other words, what is being implied is balance horizontally along the four dichotomous scales. **Balance** in type theory, however, is something altogether different.

```
                            B
                            A
        Extraversion——————————————Introversion
                            L
            Sensing——————————————Intuition
                            A
          Thinking——————————————Feeling
                            N
          Judging——————————————Perceiving
                            C
                            E
```

**Balance** in type theory is vertical, not horizontal. **Balance**, then would be balance between the Perceiving Function ("S" or "N") and the Judging Function ("T" or "F"). Because, by definition, one of these two functions is dominant in a person's type and the other is auxiliary, **Balance** could also be defined as having a dominant function working together as a team with the auxiliary. And lastly, since by definition, if the dominant is expressed in an extraverted attitude, the auxiliary is introverted, or if the dominant is expressed in an introverted attitude, the auxiliary is extraverted, **Balance** also implies a balance between the outer world and the inner world. To recap, **Balance** is vertical between the Perceiving and the Judging functions, not horizontal along lines. Indeed, if a person had several or all of his or her preferences within the "slight" category, the data may be important, but it reveals nothing at all about **Balance** (see Question 13).

It is very important that this concept be understood. Some very well known trainers muddy the waters in regard to this concept. Barr and Barr for example, in their otherwise insightful book, Leadership Equation, confuse the issue by equating "Balancing Style" with "Leadership Enhancement." By using the Jungian language, they confuse the issue, and a reader can infer that they recommend more or less equal amounts of each of the eight preferences in a successful leader. That was never Jung's intention. So what begins as a good notion—using the appropriate preference at the appropriate time—becomes flawed because of their too casual use of the word "balance."

## QUESTION 15: Can the MBTI be used for psychologically disturbed people?

The MBTI has a wellness framework. The normative work done to establish its reliability, validity, and other psychometric properties was performed on non-psychiatric audiences. Thus, any use of the MBTI with psychologically disturbed persons should be done with the understanding that the results may not be meaningful. Some individuals have done work with the indicator on persons with multiple personalities and others outside the norm. While current thinking may not include such individuals in the dysfunctional category, such use was not the intention of the indicator. There is, therefore, no reason to assume that the results are meaningful.

## QUESTION 16: Don't "TJ's" make the best top-level managers?

Frequently, the reluctance to take the Myers-Briggs Type Indicator that some individuals in organizations express to consultants stems from the fear that some of the participants are going to be told that, based on their results, they just won't make it to the top. The good news is that the indicator doesn't provide that kind of answers. No type is good; no type is bad. No type is destined to make it to the top; no type is predisposed to fail. My personal research and testing demonstrates that there are CEO's, presidents, and board chairs of the world's largest corporations in each of the sixteen squares of the type table. I have also seen the results of senior military officers in the five US Services that indicate they also select each of the sixteen types, just some with greater frequency than others. But it is one thing to say who makes the best senior managers and another to say which types tend to predominate in the upper echelons of leadership. While it looks at a slightly different sample, Ginn's and Sexton's article, "Psychological Types of *Inc.* 500 Founders and Their Spouses" (JPT, vol 16, 1988) shows that 49% of those surveyed preferred T& J.

While each of the types has shown itself capable of making it to the top, certain types do tend to predominate. The four corners of the type table ( ISTJ, INTJ, ESTJ, and ENTJ) are found in great abundance at the top echelons of leadership. Some of the firms I have worked with have in excess of 90% of their top three tiers of management in just those four descriptions. Routinely, the percentage is over 60%. The data would suggest that whatever the system, be it government, church, university, public school administration, the corporate world, or virtually any other, while all types are found in the trenches doing the actual work, about 60% of the top levels of management are found in the four corners of the type table: the "TJ's" that prompted the question. Does that frequency of appearance mean that these individuals make the best top-level managers? NO. What it means is that those who have the preference to make analytic, impersonal, objective, logical decisions based on the cause and effect relationship between the data (T's) and the preference to order, structure, schedule, and otherwise arrive at closure based on their analysis (J's), have tended to rise to the top of the corporate ladder, or to have "stuck it out" better than have most other types. These four types are those who are called the "tough-minded executives" for whom the bottom line is getting the products out the door. But, to reiterate, this fact does not mean that these individuals are the best. Empirically, that is just who we find there.

There are some trainers who, almost in a normative way, suggest that "TJ's" belong in such positions and that they are more effective in running organizations. Furthermore, they suggest that the current state of affairs, where the "TJ's" are in charge, will continue into the foreseeable future. That proposition is just an opinion, however, and I believe an unwarranted one. To make such a normative claim flies in the face of diversity and disadvantages at least twelve of the types who may make equally fine organizational leaders.

As an aside, let me speculate that that trend will not necessarily continue. Two of the multi-national corporations with which I consult are staffed by a majority of "N's" and "P's" at the top. In a global business environment that demands openness, flexibility, keen negotiating skills, and a frame of reference that says, "we must **innovate or die**," we may well find in the 1990's and on into the twenty-first century, more and more "N's," "F"s and "P's" moving into the upper ranks. (see also Rus McCarter's article, "Management and Organization Development" in the Winter, 1990 Bulletin of Psychological Type). For the moment, however, let no one be misled, *the "TJ's" are in charge!*

## QUESTION 17: How effective can the MBTI be in reflecting the "Types" of individuals from different cultures or nationalities?

It depends on what the questioner means by the MBTI. If the question is probing whether or not non-native English speakers, who are, however, fluent in English, report that the indicator has adequately reflected their preferences, the data is sparse. Most information regarding this issue is anecdotal and hinges on whether, after reading one of the type portraits on the market, the individual thinks the portrait sounds on target. I have personally administered the United States version of Forms F and G to about 200 non-native "American English" speakers from Germany, France, Taiwan, Korea, Spain, England, Australia, Turkey, New Zealand, Canada, China, the Soviet Union, Austria, Saudi Arabia, and India. The percentage of those individuals (all highly educated and fluent in English) who agreed with their reported type was substantially higher than the Manual's figures for those from the United States who agree with their reported type. In fact of the 200, only two individuals disagreed with their reported preferences (one French and one British).

The more important issue may be which version of the MBTI has a non-native English speaker taken? Jung's theory clearly is not intended just for North Americans. For a number of years Japan was the world's largest user of type theory. Now the indicator is available in several languages (26 at this printing). The only question yet to be resolved is how well the indicator has been prepared for the various countries where it is in use. One cannot *just* **translate** the English version. Indeed, one cannot even just **transliterate** it. What is vital is that the indicator be normed for the culture for which it is intended. It must be **transculturated.** I don't think you'll find that word in any dictionary. It was born out of our own work with European audiences. Some foreign language versions are trustworthy and some are not. Knowing firsthand the quality of translation and normative procedures that have gone into the German version, for example, I am confident it will be one of the best available—it may well become a standard for the industry. Some others need to be used much more cautiously. Buenas suertes!

Interest in cross-cultural applications of the MBTI is growing dramatically. There is now an International Council and an APT Cross-Cultural Committee. The Summer 1990 edition of the Bulletin of Psychological Type does the best job yet in print of summarizing much of the activity taking place around the world in regard to type.

## QUESTION 18: What are word pairs, and why do some people report this data to the client?

Some consultants, Executive Strategies International being among them, report to the client both overall preference strengths and word pair strengths if the word pairs point to a different preference from the overall. Let me explain. There are at least six separate groupings of data available to be read when a person takes the MBTI.

**Overall Scale**
Phrase Questions
**Word Pairs**
X Split-Half Score
Y Split-Half Score
Unscored questions

Of these, the ones we report to the client are the **Overall Scale** and the **Word Pairs**. The overall scale is simply the sum of the phrase questions (those that give a context to the question) and the word pairs (those that ask the client to pick a single, non-contextual word), or the sum of the X and Y split-half scores. Any one of the first five scales listed is capable of rendering type independently from the rest. The unscored questions are simply those questions that are not recorded on the scoring keys but can be studied for other issues.

The word pairs did not appear in the MBTI until Form F (166 questions). They were added because the author found that some types would read the phrase questions and instead of responding generally to their choices, would reflect back on the last time they found themselves in that situation and vote more or less specifically. Since that was not the intent of the question, the author tried to find another method of eliciting the same data. The word pairs, stripped of a context, provide that naked chance for preference. Ironically, the data indicated they were more valid than the phrase questions, but they lacked "face validity." In short, respondents didn't think they were valid. So, most of the phrase questions remain.

The reason we report the word pairs is that for some people they may provide some insights not available in just the overall score. If on the word pairs an individual reports preferences that differ from the overall score, we report that inconsistency to the client. It is additional information that may help the client better ascertain true type or understand why there may be perceived behavioral differences at different times. The Manual (p. 61) suggests three hypotheses as to what these word pairs may mean. Anyone explaining the results of the Myers-Briggs Type Indicator should stress that these are just "hypotheses." There may be more. Word pairs may give a clearer indication of how a person comes across to others spontaneously. They may also help clients see differences between their "work self" and their "at home self," or between how they see themselves and how they wish they could be.

Nechworth and Carskadon (Manual, P. 61) offer some data on the per cent of those taking the MBTI who have inconsistencies between their overall preferences and their word pairs. What the data shows is that about 75% of those tested have at least one inconsistency between phrase questions and word pairs. A current study our firm is running indicates that for those who have made it to the top echelons of organizations, the percentage of those with inconsistencies is less than 35%. Thus, the preliminary data suggests that knowing our preferences clearly may assist in helping us achieve responsible positions within organizations.

## QUESTION 19: My preference for Introversion has gotten stronger the older I have become; is that unusual?

No, not at all. There has not been much research done to explore the relationship between aging and type. In fact it is one of the real gaps in scholarship that must be corrected as we age as a culture. About all we know is that—all things being equal—our preferences tend to become clearer as we age. The one preference where we notice significant shifts is in introversion. As we age, we seem to become more comfortable with our introversion. Don't forget, introverts live in an extraverted conspiracy. The population seems to be about 70% extraverted. Thus, there is great pressure to develop extraverted skills. As we mature, we seem to become more comfortable acting on our preferences, particularly, it seems, if one of them is introversion. When this happens with clients it is often exciting to watch them finally give themselves permission to be themselves: just what Jung intended to happen.

## QUESTION 20: Are there any discernible racial differences or patterns reflected in our types?

This is a good question, and unfortunately we have precious little data upon which to draw. We face that dilemma for a number of reasons. Foremost is that nowhere on the demographic portion of the answer sheet is there a place for clients to report their races; hence, the data on types has not been kept by race, and any attempt to do so may invoke concerns as to why the question is being asked. Furthermore, even though the MBTI is reaching more and more people from diverse socio-economic and educational groupings, the normative data gathered thus far is still based predominantly on white, middle class, high school- and college-educated audiences. For this reason, any use of population percentages of the various types has to be done circumspectly.

But the question of the relationship between race and type is still broader. My experience is that those of any non-majority grouping face, perhaps more than most, the potential problem of "falsification of type" (see Question 22). To what extent do I allow environmental factors to inhibit my reporting my true preferences? Often it is the non-majority members of any organization who hear the echoes of "shape up or ship out." To a certain extent, "minorities" (this might be a person with a Boston accent in Charlotte, North Carolina) both consciously and unconsciously are drawn to report the behaviors (and perhaps the types) of the majority. Upon personal interview, these individuals sometimes admit to substantial differences between reported type and true type.

## QUESTION 21: Some consultants use letter combinations of ST, SF, NF, & NT. Others use SJ & SP in lieu of ST & SF. What is the difference?

The difference is between those who hold to a stricter **FUNCTION THEORY** approach to type and those who marry type theory with David Keirsey's observations about **TEMPERAMENT** (see *Please Understand Me*). Often the difference in practice has been prompted by where the person was trained. The Association of Psychological Type (APT) MBTI Qualifying Workshops, as do the Manual and "Introduction to Type," stress the observable characteristics of function pairs, whereas the Typewatching Qualifying Workshops offered by Otto Kroeger Associates emphasize temperament.

It is to many merely a matter of preference—which pairings give the examples of overt behavior in the clearest way. Keirsey's temperament observations, however, lack a solid appreciation of differences between extraverted and introverted attitudes and likewise suffer from the loss of the richness of Jungian theory (dominant, auxiliary, tertiary, and inferior priorities). Being a behavioralist, not a Jungian, Keirsey is unfortunately suspect in much of the Myers-Briggs community. I personally find both models useful and take different approaches depending on the typological makeup of the group I am addressing, always aware that I am on sounder theoretical underpinnings if I use function pairs rather than temperament. I must confess, however, that in business settings I see clearer differences using temperament groupings than function pairs. While Keirsey eschews any theory, his observations clearly work. When I work in educational settings, I frequently use function pairs as a means of helping clients understand differences from a behavioral perspective.

## QUESTION 22: What is meant by "falsification of type?"

"Falsification" of type can occur when individuals have allowed environmental issues—the overwhelming facticity of what developmental psychologists call "nurture"—to mask, interfere with, overwhelm, or otherwise get in the way of their reporting their genuine preferences. It may be some kind of pressure they feel to report themselves a certain way. What we are really talking about, although we shy away from using such language in MBTI circles, is faking our responses. It is a well-studied phenomenon in psychometric circles that looks at the tendency of a client to produce responses that he or she knows are necessary to fit in. Rather than be truthful, we sometimes adopt a "popular" stance instead. In more Jungian terms, one of our masks has taken over and become the person.

A serious issue, falsification of type, may interfere with a person's natural type development and hinder true individuation (see Question 23). Jung, himself, was particularly sensitive to this issue, and one of the driving forces in his psychology was the concern he felt that too often people were discouraged or prevented from becoming the persons they were truly meant to be (Manual, pp. 14-15).

## QUESTION 23: What is "individuation" and how does it differ from or relate to "good type development"?

With this question, we have moved clearly into advanced material. The terms "balance" (see Question 14), "good type development" (see Questions 4 and 22), and "individuation" are all intertwined. It is hard to discuss one without the other. Individuation is the goal of Jungian psychology—the apex of good type development—which all of us should strive for but which very few of us reach. It is, in short, the "lifelong process of becoming the complete human beings we were born to be." To use Robert A. Johnson's metaphor, it is the "actualizing of the blueprint" (*Inner Work*, p. 11). Let me explain.

On a recent consulting assignment in Europe, I had occasion to meet two German colleagues in Cologne. We agreed to meet on the steps of the main entrance to the Dom — one of the world's greatest cathedrals and architectural wonders. It is an immense gothic cathedral that dwarfs all around it and dominates the horizon of the city for miles. As you get closer, you become aware that during the construction, over hundreds of years, the style of architecture changed: spires were added, flying buttresses were expanded, great stained glass windows were commissioned and included, until what transpired was an awesome tribute to humankind's efforts to reflect, in one building, the City of Man meeting the City of God. It is as though, despite the hundreds of changes made over the centuries, a grand blueprint of what a cathedral should look like had been there all along and had finally taken form. And notice, it was not a static form. There had been a basic blueprint (you might call that "nature"), but that basic form had been modified through the years (you might call that "nurture")(see Question 1).

Well, it is just a metaphor, but a notion not too dissimilar was what Jung had in mind for individuation. He seems to have gotten the concept from Schopenhauer who talked about the principium individuationis, that seed within each living thing that determines what it was uniquely designed to be. There is, for example, something inside the tulip that says grow and become a tulip, not a tiger lily. Likewise, in each of us there is someone whom we are meant to become. The tragedy from Jung's perspective was that too many of us are forced to play roles, or wear masks, different from what our blueprints would have us to be. We become someone whom we were not intended to be—the mask, the persona, has become the person.

Another way to look at individuation is to define it as an effort to recover as much of the unconscious as possible and make it usable in a person's life. Jung would be perturbed at most of us in the Myers-Briggs community for emphasizing so much our four-letter type. I can't imagine he would appreciate at all the license plate on my car that reads **I M INTJ.** Because for Jung almost as important as our announced letters in our development are our unannounced letters—in my case, "E," "S," "F," & "P." Much of what is of value to me as an individual lies unaccessed in the unconscious. I need to access it and make it usable at the appropriate time. That means having a well-developed dominant function that has for a teammate an appropriately developed auxiliary function. While these two functions are mainly in the conscious world, they also need working with them a tertiary and an inferior function, both of which have their preponderance in the unconscious world. All four priorities are necessary for a well-developed, individuated person—one who can revel in who he or she is and not have to worry about trying to become that which he or she is not.

## QUESTION 24: How does my age affect my type?

We do not have good data on age and type. The Manual (pp. 239-41) summarizes the basic data available, but good studies on the relationship between age and type still need to be done. About all that is clear from the data is that our preferences tend to become clearer as we age (see Question 19).

Harold Grant's model (see *Facing Your Type*, p. 13) also sheds some interesting light on age and type. According to Grant, we develop, in a fairly procrustean way, our preferences as we mature. In the beginning we are relatively undifferentiated. During grade school years we work on developing what will become our dominant function. Through the years of secondary school and college, our personalities develop their auxiliary functions. Then during young adulthood we pick up interest in our tertiary functions, and around mid-life we start working on our inferior functions—that is where the fun really begins. We call that time "mid-life crisis" for good and sufficient reasons.

But a knowledge of type theory and what actually is occurring at these times in our lives can be valuable springboards for inner growth and interpersonal understanding. We could take some valuable tips from the Chinese, for whom the ideograph for "Crisis" signifies both **DANGER** and **OPPORTUNITY**. The same is true of this period in our lives when, for perhaps the first time, we begin to encounter the breadth of those functions rooted more deeply in the unconscious.

I have purposely been cavalier in describing the ages at which these various emphases occur, because I believe too many trainers are far too rigid in their approach to type development. Grant, however, is not cavalier at all but is quite specific in regard to which years relate to which priorities of our personalities.

## QUESTION 25: Why don't some psychologists accept the MBTI as a useful tool?

I suppose we all pick the experts we wish to trust, whether the question concerns the nature of God, whether to have open heart surgery or chelation therapy, or whether or not we need to take vitamins to supplement our diets. That may sound a bit "NT" or too cynical a rejoinder, but the questions are not too dissimilar. There are some psychologists who trust reliable, validated instruments to provide useful data and those who believe any such paper and pen "tests" are sheer gimmickry. Jung himself would not take the MBTI. As a clinical psychologist, he believed strongly in interview and observation as methodologies. So it is with many clinical psychologists today who are not just a little skeptical about such personality indicators.

Also, we have to realize that for a number of years Jung was not held in high favor in the psychological community. Freudians and others of non-Jungian persuasion are slow to sing the praises of a practical tool based on an "alien" theory. We also should admit that many of us who are knowledgeable in the field often spend our time working and publishing in the fields of management, teaching, and theology and have not had the impact in serious scholarly journals outside our fields of interest that we should. Thus it is only recently that articles on the MBTI have begun to appear in reputable journals of psychology.

There are also some trite uses made of the MBTI, and occasionally those using it have not been properly trained to give quality feedback to clients. Any of these problems are sufficient to raise eyebrows among serious scholars. The most popular books in the field, moreover, *Please Understand Me, Type Talk,*

*Life Types*, etc. while often entertaining and insightful, do little to advance the scholarship or research in the field, and the "data" remains anecdotal. These books are written, after all, for the layman and do not pretend to have the rigor associated with peer-reviewed scholarship. Regretfully, some trainers talk about the data they have in different areas, when the truth is they have nothing more than an intuitive feel for the data; nor do they have the means of gathering, storing, or assessing the data. We are, in short, often our own worst enemies. If there are some psychologists who are skeptical about the MBTI, it is more times than not our own fault.

## QUESTION 26: Why do different scales have different maximums?

This is a point that is sometimes missed by those who have taken the MBTI. A client may assume that a preference strength of 31 for Feeling Judgments is no more clear than a preference strength of 31 for Sensing. That simply is not the case. Because the scale for Sensing goes so much higher than the scale for Feeling Judgments, an "F" of 31 is much clearer than an "S" of 31. Unfortunately the report form provided by Consulting Psychologists Press (CPP) fails to give clients any sense of the differences in scales. It was for that reason that when I designed the report form for Otto Kroeger Associates in 1988, I placed the maximums on each scale. The ends of each scale are shaded to indicate the differing maximums. The maximums simply depend on the number of questions asked on each scale. In general, the more questions, the more reliable the scale (see Question 3). Knowing the maximum preference strength that can be associated with each of the eight preferences helps the client to see how clear one preference is when compared to the others.

But to say that the maximum limits merely reflect the number of questions asked on any one scale, really begs the question. The question that must be asked then is, "so why have a different number of questions for each scale?" The answer is not a simple one and requires an in-depth knowledge of the mechanics of setting the midpoint on the four dichotomous scales and the process used to establish the weighting of individual responses (some responses—those found on the answer keys—have weights of 1 or 2; others carry the weight of 0). The authors spent much of their adult lives ensuring the integrity of this process. The best description of how and why this took place is found in chapter ten of the Manual.

There also has to be a balance between how many questions a person might consent to answer and how many times the authors can find words and situations that reflect opposite choices with the necessary clarity. The process is not an easy one, and for this reason there is no alternative form of the indicator.

## QUESTION 27: What percentages of the population report each of the preferences?

Population percentages are tricky for a couple of reasons. First, our normative bank may be fairly skewed (see Question 20). We are just now beginning to achieve a more representative sampling. Any figures we use have to be extrapolations from those sampled. The figures in the Manual (p. 45) are dated and represent a fairly small and unrepresentative sample; nevertheless, they are quoted widely, and they have stood up pretty well through the years.

The best figures for the individual preferences come from the CAPT (Center for the Applications of Psychological Type) data bank and their ongoing Type Table Project. Like any population figures, they should be used with caution because we really do not know. The figures I use for the preferences reported by the general U. S. population are:

| | |
|---|---|
| Extravert 70% | Introvert 30% |
| Sensor 70% | Intuitive 30% |
| Thinking Judger 50% | Feeling Judger 50% |
| Judger 55% | Perceiver 45 % |

The one caveat to that data pertains to the "T"-"F" difference. Although the population seems to be split 50-50, this is the one pair that has a male-female bias. Of those who report "F," about

60 % to two thirds are female, and of those who report "T," about 60% to two thirds are male. This gender bias persists year in and year out.

Another way to sort the population by percentages is by Temperament. David Keirsey's figures are not as precise as those for the various preferences, but from Keirsey's writings one can infer the following population figures :

NT's 12 %,NF's 12 %,SJ's 38 %, SP's 38%.

Also from Keirsey we can ascertain the rough percentages for each of the types:

ISTJ, ISFJ, ISTP, ISFP—6% each
INTJ, INTP, INFJ, INFP—1% each
ESTP, ESFP, ESTJ, ESFJ—13% each
ENFP, ENTP, ENFJ, ENTJ—5% each

## QUESTION 28: How young can a person be and take the MBTI?

The Manual (pp. 6-8) describes the reading levels of the questions on Form G and F. There is more at stake, however, than just reading level. Since the questions were initially written for adult populations, the socialization level required to answer some of them is beyond any but senior high school students. Routinely, for anything other than research purposes, the MBTI ought to be administered to adult populations and older high school students only (my preference is well-functioning 10th graders and higher).

For those younger students, there is also the Murphy-Meisgeier Type Indicator for Children (MMTIC), which has been normed for children with reading levels from the second to the eighth grade (CPP is the source for this indicator as well). The MMTIC uses the same eight scales as the MBTI but has the added feature of a ninth option available on any of the four scales. The additional letter is "U" and stands for undecided, undetermined, undifferentiated, or unknown. Tied votes for any preference on the MBTI are resolved in favor of "I," "N," "F," or "P" because of the overwhelming cultural pressure to favor "E," "S," "T," or "J" (Manual, p. 156). Close scores are not resolved in the traditional manner for children, however, under the conviction that if personality growth means anything, children may opt for the preference of not preferring. Until the preference gels, the child prefers "U." The one caution regarding the indicator that is important for users to understand is that "U" is just as legitimate a choice as are the other eight preferences.

Since what is at stake is not just chronological age, but reading level and perhaps socialization level, the MMTIC can sometimes be helpful in organizations that want to use the MBTI but which have a literacy problem among its employees. The questions on the MMTIC are designed to be read to the individual answering the questions if he or she does not yet read. Thus, by using the MMTIC and the MBTI together, consultants can involve an entire plant in the process and not have to isolate those who otherwise could not read the MBTI. Of course necessary precautions must be taken to have an appropriate person read the questions and record the answers (It ought not, for example, be the person's supervisor), and the client should be informed of the original intent of the indicator because the questions were formulated with a child's experiences in mind. Despite those concerns, I have seen lives changed when persons who cannot read have been given the opportunity to participate in this way with their team members.

## QUESTION 29: Do men and women differ in how they report type?

The one noticeable difference occurs on the "T" - "F" scale (see Question 27). I would suggest that for a more thorough understanding of this difference, particularly in regard to its impact on valuing, that those interested read Carol Gilligan's superb book, *In A Different Voice*. Gilligan writes without a knowledge of type, but her comments about male and female valuing differences and misunderstandings reflects as much the "T" - "F" difference as it does the male-female difference.

## QUESTION 30: Who besides me gets my results?

Confidentiality is an important issue when discussing the results from the MBTI. The APT (Association of Psychological Type) Statement of Ethical Principles underscores several points that users of the indicator must keep in mind. Of cardinal importance is that the decision to take the indicator ought to be voluntary and that the results ought to be returned to the client only. Confidentiality, therefore, is an ethical imperative. Both internal and external consultants will have their mettle tested ensuring that this principle is upheld.

Several organizations, **ESI** included, return all results in sealed envelopes addressed to the clients individually. No one else receives the results. If, for some reason, some of the participants cannot attend the session, I keep their results until a qualified person can explain the results to them. In no event should name-tags, desk tents, type tables, or any other listing of types associated with names be prepared in advance and displayed when participants arrive.

**Each person has the right to choose whether or not to reveal his or her type, whatever the forum**.

Here's where you get to earn your money. On the one hand the consultant must honor both the letter and the spirit of this imperative to preserve the confidentiality of the results and on the other hand wants to encourage participants to be open about sharing their results. How to do this is always a challenge.

Modeling openness is a key to success. Unlike some trainers and consultants, I always announce my type from the start. It is on my business cards, my stationary, my license plate, and my lapel. If the organization has name-tags prepared in advance, I put INTJ on my name-tag as well. If there are others who appreciate type in the organization—human resources people, for example—I encourage them to announce their types as well. As I make my presentation, I am careful to underscore what type is and what it is not, and through a series of personal anecdotes—oftentimes humorous ones— about my friends, family, business associates, and experiences help audiences experience the excitement and non-threatening nature of the results (eg, no bad types, no good types; no smart types, no dumb types; no sick types, no well types; no types suited to the job, no types not suited to the job).

If the consultant has done this well, by the time participants receive their results, they are anxious to share them with those sitting around them. "Yea, I knew it; I guessed three of the four letters. I'm an ESTJ. What are you?" And the banter begins. It is at this point that I ask those who are comfortable doing so to sign in on a large type table I have posted somewhere to the rear of the room. As you send them out for a break, the chart starts to fill. I am careful to stress, however, that there is no obligation whatsoever to share their types.

If, during the presentation, I show a type table of the organization to the group, it will be so they can see how many others of the same or different types there are in the organization. The type table is always devoid of names and gender and merely reflects numbers or percentages of the types or combinations of letters (eg, ST, SF, NF, NT). There are even some times when showing such a generic, scrubbed, type table may be inappropriate—with very small groups for example, where by virtue of sheer numbers one could guess someone's type. No master list of names and types is prepared, and no one receives the results except the individual clients. You will be pressured to do so from time to time, and you must decline, citing your ethical obligations and the individual's rights to confidentiality. That has been your contract with the individual, and you must allow no one to void that contract for you.


## QUESTION 31: How can knowing my type or the types of others foster better communications?

If you and I see reality differently, we can't have a meaningful conversation. If you and I make our judgments seeing the data through different lenses, we have a hard time understanding one another's positions. If I speak French and you speak Japanese, we have to work very hard, often through non-verbal means to understand one another. If East and West Germans did not have a common language and heritage, reunification would not have occurred as swiftly as it did. Learning about type is, to some degree, analogous to learning to communicate in other languages. Consider this basic cybernetic model of communication.

```
          MESSAGE ——>       s              D
             N              t      MESSAGE ——>
             C              a              C
SENDER       O           MEDIUM           O        RECEIVER
             D              t              D
          MESSAGE ——>       i      MESSAGE ——>
             R              c              R
```

In any communication system, between NASA and the space shuttle or between you and your employees, there is the sender, the message, the receiver, and the medium through which the message is sent. The message may be a thirty-minute marketing presentation, E-Mail, an inter-office memo, a counseling session, feedback on an evaluation report, or an award for twenty years of faithful service. In any event, each time a message is sent, it is encoded at the sender's end and decoded at the receiver's end.

When you send a message via E-mail, you encode it mechanically at the keyboard, the computer encodes what you say into computer language, the message is sent electronically, and the reverse procedure occurs at the other end, as the message is decoded and made understandable to the receiver. Here's where type plays such an important role in communication.

When you and I have a conversation, I as an INTJ encode my view of reality in "N." I encode my judging style in "T." If you happen to be an ESFJ, you decode my message in "S" and "F." Unless we understand the differences, we can't talk. The message is garbled; static scrambles the meaning, and you decode the message using the wrong code book. Simply stated, the receiver must use the same protocol as the sender. If they don't, there is no communication. That happens every day in your organization and mine. We need to develop skills in presenting material to others in ways that they can best understand, otherwise we communicate only at shallow levels and often misinterpret others.

One approach I use in organizations to underscore this important concept is to teach people how to make presentations to those of other types. Structuring data in specific ways or presenting concepts with clarity involves knowing the preferred style of the person receiving the information. To do less is to risk a lack of understanding or at worst to have a proposal rejected.

## QUESTION 32: Which types work together best on a team?

Without being prescriptive, about all we can say is that some types are more likely to work together with harmony than others; that's another way of saying there may be a more natural kinship among some types than others. My personal preference, born of experience but substantiated by theory, is that people who have two letters in common, one of which is one of the middle two, make the best partners, teammates, co-trainers, etc. By matching one of the middle two letters, we are sure that the two have at least either their dominant or auxiliary function in common (see Question 40). That kinship, however, *guarantees* nothing.

It may also be possible to group different types for different results. I discuss some of those specific groupings in my book on teambuilding.

## QUESTION 33: If I am under pressure when I fill out the indicator, will my results be valid?

This is one question that you can not answer. Only the client can. As consultants, we *never* know if the indicator has identified the person's true preferences. That is why self-validation of type is so important. As a general response, you can alert the client to the fact that there may be several reasons why the reported type may not reflect true type (see Questions 2 and 22). Pressure is one of them. A person under stress may not report true type. My experience, however, is that this aberration is rare, and that even at such times the indicator is sophisticated enough to come close. **The client**, though, **is the final authority**.

## QUESTION 34: Can I tell from their MBTI preferences which of my employees will be honest or dishonest?

NO! Fortunately the MBTI does not measure such things as honesty or dishonesty, right or wrong, sick or well. If it did, few clients would fill it out. Different types do tend to approach values and ethical decision making differently. I discuss these differing typological approaches to values in the chapter on ethics in my teambuilding book.

## QUESTION 35: I know you have said that there are no good types and no bad types, but, honestly, don't "P's" procrastinate more than "J's"?

This is one of those questions where my answer has tended to change over the years. One of my early mentors in type taught me to say that procrastination is not particularly a "P" issue—that all of us procrastinate around our non-preferences (*Type Talk*, p. 93). I believed that for some time and even argued it diligently while teaching in Qualifying Workshops despite frequent evidence to the contrary. I no longer share that perspective. In an effort to affirm all preferences as valuable, and indeed they are, I believe he stretched the meaning of the word "procrastinate." Indeed "P's" do procrastinate. They admit it; why shouldn't the "J's"?

To procrastinate is to put off until a later time. All of us at least appear to do that in different aspects of our lives. The introverted intuitive judger, for example, is sometimes experienced as a "P" for this very reason. For example, some time ago I was asked to write an article on ethics for a scholarly journal. My deadline to have the article at the publisher was about three weeks away on a Monday. I had been thinking about what I was going to say for some time but had not yet put pen to paper. The conceptual work was going on inside, but no words were hitting the paper. My wife was worried and my publisher was a little irked by my "procrastination." But what she read as procrastination was real work going on out of sight. The deadline for my article was on a Monday. The Saturday before the article was due, my daughter and I were running on the beach. Suddenly I stopped and began writing in the sand with a stick. My 12-year old INTP daughter, who had seen similar behavior before, said, "Oh, so the ideas finally gelled?" Indeed they had. I returned home, wrote the article, and faxed it before supper on Sunday. Deadlines are, after all, deadlines to a "J." Not necessarily to a "P," for whom deadlines are sometimes *signals to begin.*

While the "P" in the type formula does not stand for **Procras**tinate, "P's" do have a special knack for getting on "J's" nerves by putting things off. There is, after all, so much data for a "P" to consider. "Ps" run around much like the robot-turned-human, Johnny 5, in the movie, "Short Circuit," saying, "OOOO, INPUT!" As the "P" for perceiver suggests, "P's" externalize their perceiving function (either sensing or intuition) and allow the rest of us to benefit from their perceptions. That can be quite helpful in organizations where the tendency is often to get something, anything, done, often without "wasting time" considering all that "extraneous" information. As a result, sometimes all we see are the frustrations associated with the differences.

A friend tells this story about his family. Last Christmas, his "J" daughter asked her "P" mother a simple question: "Mom, can we string cranberries for the Christmas tree this year?" He sat out in his study hearing the question and thought, what a nice homey question. The nuclear family is intact and all is well in the world. Then his "P" wife proceeded to answer the question. "That's a great question, Honey. We haven't strung cranberries for a long time. I remember, years ago we used to string cranberries all the time. In fact sometimes we would string popcorn and other times cranberries; sometimes we would mix the two. Then, again, we also used to bring the tree in much earlier from the forest. But that's because houses were much colder then than they are now. We didn't have central heating systems and sometimes just used a stove or a fireplace in one room. So the tree would last longer and not lose its needles or become a fire hazard. That also meant that fruit on the tree would keep much longer and not go bad because of the excessive heat. In fact homes were sometimes so cool that people kept all kinds of fresh food in the cellar. Sometimes there were pickle barrels and even dried meat hanging from the rafters. If there was just a dirt floor in the basement, sometimes people even dug holes in the floors and buried potatoes or beets in the ground to keep them fresh during the winter. . . ."

For fifteen minutes, the "P" gave the "J" the history of food in America. When she was all finished, the "J" daughter said: "So Mom, can we string cranberries on the tree this year?" The wife said, "I just told you we could!" To the "J," she hadn't even come close. Because the "J" externalizes the judging function and expects closure and certainty in the answer, YES or NO are the appropriate choices. The "P" thought she had "answered the mail." The "J" knew otherwise.

With all the other functions, the word "procrastinate" is inappropriate. We do not "procrastinate" around our non-preferences; they simply rate further down on our list of priorities. The "S" avoids theory and concept; the "N" avoids the detailed approach. The "T" avoids interpersonal involvement; the "F" avoids critical comment and impersonal analysis. Procrastination is a different issue. Ironically, sometimes precisely because we know some approaches or activities are non-preferences, we choose to do them first, but because we have not had much practice doing them they come across as awkward or childish.

On a trip to Arkansas some months ago, I worked with a company headed by a "P." His immediate staff were all "J's." We met for supper at 6:00 pm. During supper, they began to discuss how they should arrange the golf foursomes the next day after my presentation. By midnight, the "P" boss had still not agreed to the various suggestions that had been made. One of the "J's" turned to me before we broke for the night and said, "Bill, you really have your work cut out for you tomorrow. What you just saw is a pattern of every staff meeting we have had for the last two months since he took over."

What the "J" didn't realize yet, was the strength the "P" brought to the organization by preventing premature closure, by encouraging a sorting out of the options. All she saw was the procrastination, and that she saw negatively. Therein lies probably the greatest tension in organizations: **"J"s vs. "P"s.** I have had "P"s admit, "You know Bill, my colleagues think I am downright irresponsible. I simply can't structure my life to meet their expectations."

When properly exercised the "P" is vital to the organization. When there is too much of it, it can enervate. It's much like the old Greek concept of the tragic flaw in drama. The great tragic heroes of ancient literature did not fail because of some sin, vice, or weakness. Their fault was their Hamartia —their "tragic flaw" was defined as an **excess of virtue.** The "J" attitude is a virtue. The "P" attitude is a virtue. But while both are potential virtues, an excess of either one can be a real detriment to organizational effectiveness.

## QUESTION 36: As an ENFP, why do I have such a hard time introducing myself to others or sharing personal insights during presentations? Aren't I supposed to be gregarious and friendly?

We occasionally assign behavioral characteristics to types based on assumptions about one or two letters, when in fact those assumed behaviors do not really match our preferences. Such superficiality is unfortunate. The ENFP is not alone in this regard, but the question takes us to the heart of type theory. For each type there is, theoretically, a priority according to which we prefer to use our functions: we refer to them as follows:

**Dominant**—most preferred, most comfortable, most trustworthy

**Auxiliary**—second most preferred, second most comfortable

**Tertiary**—third most preferred, third most comfortable

**Inferior**—least preferred, least comfortable, most uncontrollable

Each of these functions is also expressed in a characteristic attitude, either extraverted or introverted. All those who are knowledgeable in the field of type agree as to the attitudes of the dominant, auxiliary, and inferior functions. For all extraverted types, the dominant function is extraverted and the auxiliary and the inferior functions are introverted. For all introverts, the dominant function is introverted and the auxiliary and the inferior functions are extraverted.

Where the disagreement exists is in regard to the attitude in which the tertiary function is expressed. Those who authored the Manual hold to the view that the tertiary function is introverted for extraverts and extraverted for introverts (p. 18). I, along with Grant, Clark, Thompson, Kroeger, and others disagree. We hold to the view that the tertiary function is always "in the same attitude as the dominant function" (Manual, p. 294, note 10). For us the attitudes are expressed as follows:

| ALL EXTRAVERTS | ALL INTROVERTS |
|---|---|
| **DOMINANT**—Extraverted | **DOMINANT**—Introverted |
| **AUXILIARY**—Introverted | **AUXILIARY**—Extraverted |
| **TERTIARY**—Extraverted | **TERTIARY**—Introverted |
| **INFERIOR**—Introverted | **INFERIOR**—Extraverted |

Experientially, the view represented in the Manual makes no sense to me or to those whom I know. Theoretically, the issue of balance in type theory also leads me to my view. If one way to see balance is to see it as teamwork between the extraverted attitude and the introverted attitude for the dominant and the auxiliary (see Question 14), by extension it would seem logical (I am a "T") that the same balance should exist between the attitudes of the tertiary and the inferior functions ( eg, that one should be expressed in the introverted attitude and one should be expressed in the extraverted attitude). There needs to be balance among those functions predominantly in the unconscious as well as those predominantly in the conscious part of our personality.

But to be candid, the tertiary function is the one we know the least about, hence, the confusion about its attitude. There are even some who ride the fence here and aver that the tertiary function can have either attitude. This is simply one aspect of type theory on which scholars disagree.

All this is prologue to the question about the ENFP. For the ENFP, the following priorities apply:

**Dominant**—intuition
**Auxiliary**—feeling judgments
**Tertiary**—thinking judgments
**Inferior**—sensing

By either schema of assigning attitudes to the four functions, the feeling function for the ENFP is introverted, whereas the intuitive function is extraverted. Even though David Keirsey has colored all of our views about the ENFP as gregarious, happy-go-lucky, and personable, the feeling judgments—that interpersonal function—is both introverted and auxiliary, and thus we may not see it, and the ENFP may feel ill at ease "going public" with that side of his or her personality.

## QUESTION 37: I hear people talk about "working out of their shadow function." What does that mean?

It means they are confused about the difference between the "shadow" and the "inferior function." The inferior is a function rooted predominantly in the unconscious, which when we use it or have to fall back on it, can cause some rocky times. The shadow is not a function — not a preference; the shadow is an archetype. The difference is keen. It is, by definition, our least preferred function, but under a lot of stress we sometimes revert to using it. Unless we are well developed in type and relatively individuated (see Question 23), we can come across as out of control and fairly primitive in our behavior.

The shadow, however, is an archetype. That means it resides in the unconscious as a pool of potentiality. Archetypes are universal paradigms of meaning, action, possibilities, and energy that the human race has in common. As Johnson tells us, while they are universal, "they combine in infinite variations to create individual human psyches" (*Innerwork*, p. 11). As with all archetypes, the shadow has both universal applicability and individual selectivity. Unfortunately, the very words we associate with "shadow" are dark, sinister, evil, unknown, lurking, etc. so that we get an eerie feeling about its potential in our lives. It can, however, have a positive, catalytic effect in our lives as long as we "deal with it" on our terms—as Jung suggested we must. If it comes to play on its terms, we are not at all at ease.

In short, however, one does not "work out of" his or her shadow. One only works out of functions. The one closest to the shadow, the one through which the shadow is most likely to appear, is the inferior. One can work out of his or her inferior. Unfortunately, too many people confuse the two.

## QUESTION 38: How often should I take the MBTI?

It depends on why you are taking it. Probably the first time a person takes the indicator—untainted by what the choices might imply—it is, all things being equal, the best look at one's preferences. Each time thereafter, as one's knowledge of what is being asked increases, there is a greater risk that consciously or unconsciously a person can skew the results. As more and more training programs for employees, programs for executives, in-service workshops for teachers, and others find the MBTI to be the valuable tool it is, people will be taking and retaking the indicator.

Each time a person fills out the indicator, the data can be revealing. Did the results change or stay the same? What happened to your results after the divorce, job change, departure of your daughter to college, pink slip, separation from service, promotion, or mid-life crisis? Particularly because we tend to develop more fully our priority of preferences as we grow older (see Questions 19, 23, & 24), subsequent retakes can prove enlightening. If you are taking it more than a couple of times a year, however, except as part of training programs, you may be into too much self-analysis. Maybe it's time to get on with life.

## QUESTION 39: Can't I come out any type I want to on the MBTI?

Certainly the more a person understands type theory, psychometrics, and what preferences the various questions are attempting to sort out, the easier it is to answer the questions in accordance with the answers expected from different types. Those persons preferring "N" and "T" seem to have a particular knack for doing this, if not a drive to do so. But to try "to game" the answers flies in the face of reasons for taking the indicator.

First and foremost, the MBTI is a self-assessment instrument. It may be valuable to be able to understand colleague's behaviors, learning styles, communication styles, and the raft of issues we use the MBTI for, but the principal use it has is to foster self understanding. Trying to come out any type we want to may be good sport for certain types, but it begs the question of why we take the MBTI to begin with.

Just as an aside, while it is possible to skew the results, picking a type and answering the questions accordingly is more difficult than might be expected. I have had several people with impressive credentials attempt to do this, and few have succeeded. The indicator is remarkably sophisticated.

## QUESTION 40: Is any one of my four letters more important or more influential than the others?

Just as a corporation needs a leader and a ship needs a captain, so the personality needs a boss. According to the theory, each of us early in life selects a preference that Jung called the Dominant or the Superior function to be in charge of the personality. Theoretically, it is our most favored, most accessible, most trustworthy, and if all has gone well, our best developed function. Isabel Briggs Myers called it the "General" of the personality (*Gifts Differing*, p. 14). The description in *Gifts Differing* is the most accessible explanation available for understanding this function and how to discover which it is in each of the types (see also Question 36).

Which function is dominant is not arrived at by finding the preference with the clearest strength; it is arrived at theoretically depending on the person's reported preferences for the two attitudes. There may be a number of reasons why a person may report a clearer preference for the auxiliary than for the dominant.

*The following are the dominant functions for each type*

For ISTJ, ISFJ, ESTP, and ESFP, the **dominant** function is **Sensing**

For INFJ, INTJ, ENFP, and ENTP, the **dominant** function is **Intuition**

For ISTP, INTP, ESTJ, and ENTJ, the **dominant** function is **Thinking**

For ISFP, INFP, ESFJ, and ENFJ, the **dominant** function is **Feeling**

Each of these four groupings will look different in behavior as well as sharing different interests. Furthermore, the differences will depend on whether the dominant function is expressed in the extraverted or the introverted attitude. With that added dimension, we have moved onto Jungian turf with eight groupings. The Manual does a fine job outlining the differences one can expect from these Jungian groupings (pp. 22-29).

## QUESTION 41: Can I use the MBTI to hire the right employee for a job?

The APT (Association of Psychological Type) Statement of Ethical Principles makes it clear that psychological type ought not to be used to advantage or disadvantage anyone. Clearly, by that wisdom, it should not be used as the criteria for hiring or firing anyone. Moreover, not only would it be improper to hire someone based solely upon type, it would also be irresponsible. Let's say there was a job in my organization that by some process I knew was the perfect job for an ESTJ. I would much rather hire a smart INFP (a four letter opposite) than a dull ESTJ, an ethical INTP than an unethical ESFJ, a mature ISTP than a childish ENFJ, and the list could go on.

Since type reveals nothing about such parameters—it measures only preferences—it is a poor criterion for hiring or firing or promoting or demoting. On the pragmatic side, should you decide to hire someone or not hire someone based on type, you are likely to have a class action suit filed against you. The predictive nature of the MBTI on specific job performance has not been demonstrated adequately.

## QUESTION 42: Should I use my type to choose a career?

It all depends on what you mean by "use." If you mean should ISTJ's become accountants, INTJ's become CEO's, INTP's become scientists, ENFJ's become ministers, and ESTJ's become foremen, the answer is a resounding No! Can type be helpful in choosing a career? Definitely yes!

All of us have a number of talents and capabilities, likes and dislikes, not dependent on type. To use our types to pick our careers is to limit who we are. There are a number of listings of types by career field. The Manual (pp. 243-292) is one of the best. The chapter on Career Counseling (pp. 77-93) also contains some valuable advice.

Where type can be extremely useful in career choices is in seeing where our interests match the career fields we are considering. Thus taking the MBTI as a college student or high school student can often prove quite beneficial. Where those interests match, the client is much more likely to find that career enjoyable. However, that match in no way guarantees success in the particular job. Empirically, we *can* say where different types are likely to wind up. There is clearly much self-selection that occurs in terms of careers. But the fact that many of the same type can be found in the same job does not imply that they are either suited to that job or that they are doing quality work.

Should a person decide to choose a career where very few or none of his or her type are represented, that person may very well have an uphill battle fitting in. On the plus side, however, that person probably has the greatest possible contribution to make.

In short, knowledge of type can be quite valuable in looking at careers to see where a person may find a greater comfort level. It should not, however, be used to steer persons toward or away from any career or profession. That is an improper use of type.

## QUESTION 43: Does being an "F" mean that I am more emotional than my "T" associates?

No, not necessarily. Jung did not intend for the term feeling judger, "F," to be associated with emotions any more than he intended for the term thinking judger, "T," to be linked with intelligence. Emotions may well help the "F" to decide rationally just as logic may help the "T" to decide rationally, but persons with either preference may be emotional or unemotional. Both "T" and "F" are what Jung called the "rational functions." If I were to link "being emotional" with any set of preferences, I would tie it to the attitudes of introversion and extraversion. Extraverted "T"s, for example, can be much more "emotional" than many introverted "F"s.

Also at stake is in which attitude the "F" function is expressed. For example, the ENFP (see Question 36), while extraverted as a type, has, as an auxiliary function, introverted feeling judgments. The ESFJ, on the other hand, while extraverted, extraverts feeling judgments as the dominant function. All things being equal, the ESFJ comes across as much more "emotional" than the ENFP, yet both are "E's" and both are "F's." The INFJ, while introverted, extraverts the auxiliary function — "F". The INFP introverts the same function, even though for the INFP "F" is dominant. On par, the INFJ is much more "emotional" than the INFP, who can often be one of the cooler types. And, to complicate things further, just about any "ET" can come across as more "emotional" than any "IF."

In sum, no, being an "F" does not mean a person is more emotional than a "T" colleague.

## QUESTION 44: Sixteen letters are a lot to remember. Do you have any tips for remembering what all these letters mean?

You're right. Many of the programs that consultants use to assist organizations are based on systems of threes or fours. Their virtue is that they are relatively easy to remember. The MBTI uses eight distinct variables that are grouped into sixteen possible personality types. Furthermore, these letters are treated in a number of different pairings when attempting to demonstrate behavioral characteristics. While these letters and meanings make the MBTI more complex as a system and potentially harder to remember, the possibilities inherent are manyfold more. It does, however, take longer to understand the system. One way to appreciate the contribution made by each letter and the overall impact of a four-letter type is a visual model we use at Executive Strategies International. Each of the sixteen types can be expressed as the following *Type*-o-graphics. First, a word of explanation.

*Type*-o-graphics offers a concise representation of how our four preferences relate to each other. By determining the purpose of each letter and how it interreacts with the other three, we can develop a better understanding of type.

* The first of the four letters of our type determines where we get our **ENERGY**:

From the outer world " ⮀ E " or
from the inner world "I ⮀ " .

* The second letter denotes **how we see reality** and **gather information**:
    straightforward / realistic "S——"or
    abstract / considering possibilities

    "N ⟵ ", "N ⬯— ". ** (See J/P line)

* The third letter indicates **how we make our decisions,** whether our judging process is influenced by
    **feeling** judgments - "F" or
    **thinking** judgments - "T".

* The fourth letter represents our **lifestyle,** whether that be more prone to

    **CLOSURE** - "J" or
    **OPENNESS** - "P".

** (When combined with "N", the possibility lines go to closure for "J" and remain open for "P".)

# *Type* - o- graphics

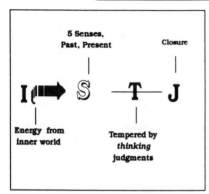

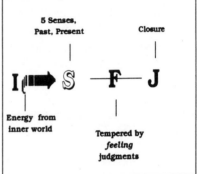

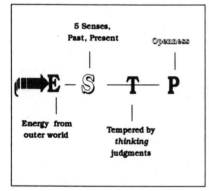

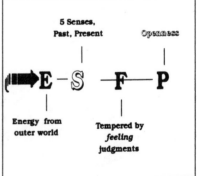

## *Dominant SENSING*

# *Type* - o- graphics

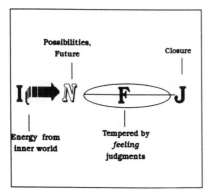

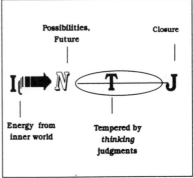

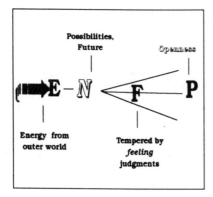

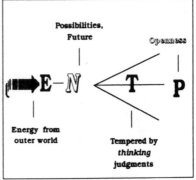

## *Dominant* **INTUITION**

© *1990 Executive Strategies International*

# *Type* - o- graphics

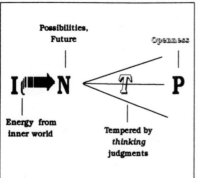

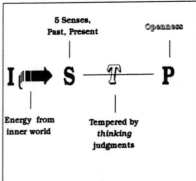

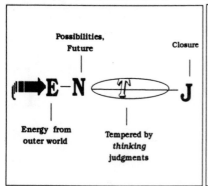

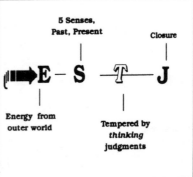

# *Dominant THINKING*

## *Type* - o- graphics

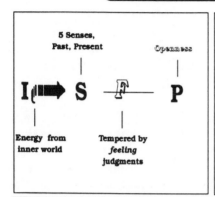

5 Senses,
Past, Present

Openness

I ➡ S — *F* — P

Energy from
inner world

Tempered by
*feeling*
judgments

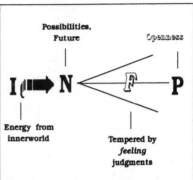

Possibilities,
Future

Openness

I ➡ N — *F* — P

Energy from
innerworld

Tempered by
*feeling*
judgments

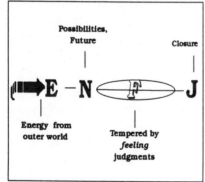

Possibilities,
Future

Closure

➡ E – N — *F* — J

Energy from
outer world

Tempered by
*feeling*
judgments

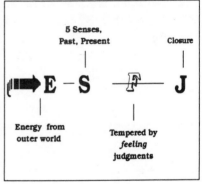

5 Senses,
Past, Present

Closure

➡ E – S — *F* — J

Energy from
outer world

Tempered by
*feeling*
judgments

## *Dominant FEELING*

© *1990 Executive Strategies International*

## QUESTION 45: How am I likely to act in regard to my type when I am under stress?

Experts in the field disagree regarding how stress may affect the behavior normally expected from a type. My experience is that when we undergo stress, we tend to fall back on what we know best. We retreat to our comfort zone. In type that corresponds to our preferences; we fall back on our strengths to combat the stress. In particular, we may fall back on our dominant function and trust it more than usual. So, under stress, an INTJ becomes the paradigm of the INTJ; the ESTP becomes the paradigm of the ESTP, and so on.

But when we confront **major stress**, the routine can go haywire, and type alone may become inadequate. At these times we may slip from strength to weakness. Rather than fall back on our preferences, we tend to resort to our non-preferences and can actually wind up acting out of our inferior function. The bad news is that when we act out of our inferior function, we tend to act more immaturely, more primitively, more childishly, and out of control.

Clearly, stress can skew our results when filling out the indicator. The degree of stress we are under, however, may well determine how we might behave. When we see someone under major stress, we often say, "Oh, she's not acting herself today." In terms of type, she quite profoundly may *not* be herself today.

## QUESTION 46: I have seen some recent criticism of the MBTI that suggests that it is little more than a quaint parlor game because all it indicates is positive traits about a person. What do you say?

Remember that the MBTI is a *preference* indicator. Preferences are by their very nature not susceptible to categories of right or wrong. It is not that the indicator just picks up on positive traits, but that those leading workshops on type or giving individual feedback sessions to clients may tend to emphasize just the positive characteristics of each type. That should be the starting point because the hallmark of type is that it helps to affirm the intrinsic worth of each individual, but as a follow-on, clients must come to respect that for every strength there may be a concomitant weakness.

The ISTJ's keen sense of responsibility, for instance, may, taken to extremes, result in authoritarianism, rigidity, or misdirected compulsiveness. The ESTJ's straight-shooting, up-front approach to issues may, taken to extremes, become confrontational and abrasive. The ENTP's knack for pushing the boundaries and generating new and creative ideas, can result in their breeding stress in organizations. The desire to nurture, to help, to care, that we associate with the INFP, can result in guilt because they themselves may not live up to their own passionate idealism. The ENTJ's almost instinctive ability to lead can, when improperly exercised, become dogmatic and blustering.

Yes, there are strengths associated with each of the types. Yes, a knowledge of type helps us to learn to cherish diversity. But we dare not be myopic. There are also potential quagmires we all have to avoid. The indicator is faithful in reporting preferences. We must be faithful in interpreting the results.

## QUESTION 47: Is there an ideal sequence of events when presenting a feedback session to a group of people?

Yes, and here I am indebted to a number of nameless people, students, colleagues, and friends, who have heard me experiment with different approaches over the last nine years and didn't complain and to a number of other professionals in the field whose presentations I have heard and evaluated over the years. The approach I use is suitable to virtually any audience but particularly to the business community.

I prefer a full day to introduce the MBTI to an audience and to have an in-house resource available to help with any follow-on work that might be necessary. The latter often is not available, and the time I am allotted is occasionally much less. What I will describe, therefore, is an approach suitable to a half-day introduction to the MBTI. That time frame is the norm for most organizations.

I begin with some general observations:

1. The unique language I will be introducing (eg, extraversion, introversion, sensing, intuition, etc).

2. What the MBTI *is not* and what it *is*.

3. A brief description of the psychometric properties of the indicator. I limit this to a few comments about the reliability and the validity of the indicator.

4. A brief explanation of the theory—Jung's belief that there are two primary forms of mental functioning and what that understanding suggests about how we perceive and judge.

I next get quite specific and make the bulk of the presentation as practical as I can (see Question 50 for details). This section includes

5. I begin with an overview of the eight preferences. CAPT has some excellent viewgraphs that can assist you in this regard; they are black and white stick figures with appropriate comments. **Executive Strategies International** also offers a superb package of colored view graph transparencies to support your presentation. This section is the heart of the presentation. I routinely discuss the eight preferences for about two hours, grounding the entire time in anecdotes about myself, my associates, and those with whom I have worked in the past. This approach not only roots the presentation practically, but it also models the openness I hope will result as people begin voluntarily to discuss their types.

6. At this point I return the participants' results. Each person gets a report form in a sealed envelope to reinforce the obligation I feel toward confidentiality. I also remind them that no one else gets a copy of their results, and they are free to reveal or not to reveal their results as they see fit.

So far they have not had their results in front of them. I do this for two reasons. First, I want the participants to be guessing, as the presentation unfolds, what their reported types might be. Not only does this help me to evaluate the quality of my presentation, but it also, and most importantly, helps the participants to come to terms with the possible differences between reported type and true type (see Questions 2, 5, and 22). The second reason is that were I to hand out the results before I begin, the odds are that participants would tend to focus *just* on their preferences and not on the other four. Since from my perspective, the basic reason for people to take the MBTI is to help understand themselves and others, I want people to focus on all eight preferences, not just their own.

7. Here is an ideal place to have some of the participants volunteer to participate in exercises that will highlight the differences I have been discussing. I use exercises that point out the differences between the dichotomous pairs. Nothing helps more than this process to underscore the validity of the results and to help those whose preferences are not clear to gain some clarity about their choices.

8. I then show a type table, by number or percentage only, of all the types represented in the audience.

9. I conclude with an exercise and some comments that reinforce some behavioral considerations around letter combinations, either function pairs or temperament (see Question 21).

10. Finally, I conclude with some warnings about what is likely to happen as a result of our time together. **What would be ideal is that participants begin to cherish diversity** not just give lip service to it. What may happen, however, is that we turn loose on the world a group of zealous amateur psychologists who begin to type everyone and everything in sight. They need to have reinforced the fact that such is not the goal of the indicator and that they do not have the skill or a complete enough understanding of the model to make such judgments.

I have used this same approach hundreds of times and have found it to work. I would strongly suggest using as many visual aids (overhead transparencies, slides, and flip charts) as possible. Those with sensing preferences tend to learn best in this way. As a general rule, intuitives can learn from a sensing approach easier than sensors can learn from an intuitive approach. When in doubt about the make-up of the group, therefore, aim for the sensors. Of course the ideal approach, the one I always request from clients, is that you know which types are present before you begin the presentation. That way you can structure the presentation accordingly.

**QUESTION 48: You have discussed a great number of the benefits one derives from taking the MBTI, but what is the downside? What possible negative consequences can occur when organizations use the MBTI?**

This is a great question because while it isn't always asked, it always seems to be lurking in the shadows. Here are some concerns that we often overlook in our zeal to have people take the MBTI. Any time we use instrumentation of any kind in small groups we open ourselves up to certain disadvantages

1. There is always the **fear of exposure**. What does this say about me? Who is going to know? Why are we filling out this form and the office down the hall is not? Are we downsizing again or removing another layer of middle management based on our results? This kind of institutional paranoia is always possible and should be tackled head-on by the consultant (see Questions 16, 30, and 4).

2. Such instrumentation encourages "labeling." This is always a possible consequence and one to be avoided. Of course we already do this quite well. I encourage audiences to think about the ways they already label people in damaging ways. All retired military think like..., all southerners are..., all women with short hair..., all men with beards are..., all Italians, all blacks, all.... And the list goes on. So, long before people know anything about psychological type, they are involved in the very human and often damaging activity of labeling other people. In many ways type cuts across those labels and helps us to see value where there might just be stereotype.

3. Such instrumentation can result in information overload. This objection is certainly valid. There is much to understand about the MBTI and Jungian theory. Frequently consultants will overwhelm audiences with the sheer bulk of information or complexity of the system. Consultants and trainers must be sensitive to this issue and know what to communicate and what not to say in a half-day, full-day, or two-day session. Some types reach data overload faster than others. We need to be sensitive to this potential problem.

4. "Testing" can trigger anxiety and even anger from the "school" connotation. For this reason, participants should be alerted prior to filling out the indicator to the non-threatening nature of the MBTI. It is, in fact, an "indicator," not a "test." As long as participants think about the indicator as a test, there will be rights and wrongs associated with the answers. We all learned in school what it felt like to fail or at least to do less well than a friend on a test. To pre-empt the fear of getting results back, we must be clear about what the MBTI really is.

5. It may be seen as diverting from key issues. Frequently I hear from a client something like, "are we going to begin team building on the retreat or just do something that makes us feel good?" There is the assumption that the link between instrumentation and "real" staff development may be spurious at best. I make it clear that nothing is more central to teambuilding than self-knowledge. Even if we stop at that point during a retreat, it is a real plus for an organization. Of course, we go much further, but we start with the individual and then branch out to the others he or she touches in the organization. Perhaps I am overdramatic at times in stating it this way, but I remind audiences of Jung's concern with the whole person and say, "If you are going to die of a heart attack before the age of 45, you are worthless to the organization; if you are unethical, you are worthless to the organization; if you don't really know yourself, you are worthless to the organization." That's the practical foundation for the MBTI.

So, yes, there are possible disadvantages that may arise from the use of the MBTI in organizations. If, however, we are responsible in the use of the instrument, and if we communicate the correct information to participants both before and after they fill it out, the advantages by far outstrip the possible disadvantages. Here are just a few clear advantages of the use of instrumentation—whatever the form—in small groups:

1. Enables early, easy learning of a theory
2. Promotes personal involvement
3. Develops early understanding of constructs and terminology
4. Supplies personal feedback earlier than otherwise possible
5. Produces personal commitment to information and feedback
6. Facilitates contracting for new behaviors among participants

7. Fosters open reception of feedback through low threat environment

8. Provides for comparisons of individuals with others and norm groups

9. Promotes involvement with data and feedback process

10. May surface latent issues

11. Allows facilitators to focus and control the group behavior appropriately.

12. Facilitates assessment of change over a period of time. This is particularly true if the indicator is used in conjunction with any kind of organizational assessment such as the one developed at ESI.

## QUESTION 49: Is there any significance to the order in which the letters in the type formula appear?

The letters could have appeared in any order at all, but their current order reflects in part the development of the theory. For Jung, the chief discriminator was extraversion and introversion. It seems only appropriate, therefore, that "E" or "I" should begin the formula. Similarly, Jung said there were two primary forms of mental functioning—perception and judgment. Thus, the perceiving function, "S" or "N," comes second, and the judging function, "T" or "F," follows in the third spot. Since the "J" - "P" distinction was added by the authors of the indicator, it is only appropriate that it should occupy the fourth spot. So, while there is nothing magic about the ordering of the letters, their sequence reflects much of the theory.

## QUESTION 50: How can I best describe the MBTI and the associated preferences to an audience? What, exactly, should I use as examples?

As you hear a number of different presentations by experts in the field, you will find a style that best suits you. You also, no doubt, will begin to collect stories and examples that will highlight the different preferences in ways that will bring the material alive to the most ardent critic. The answer to Question 47 discusses the general sequence of events in a good MBTI presentation. The following section that underscores what the MBTI *IS* and *IS NOT* offers some specific suggestions as to the kind of examples I use in my presentations. It is also a good review of the basics of type theory and may be the best place to begin if your understanding of type could use a refresher before grappling with the more difficult questions you are likely to receive. GOOD LUCK!

# WHAT IT IS AND WHAT IT ISN'T

The Myers-Briggs Type Indicator (MBTI) is a carefully validated, highly reliable personality inventory that allows individuals to declare the degree to which they express preferences for eight aspects of human personality. It is not, as many consultants and popularizers of the indicator refer to it, a psychological *test*. The distinction is important, even though the word "test" is used popularly to describe several such instruments, because the word suggests that the choices on the MBTI are somehow related to categories of right or wrong.

Perhaps no feature of the MBTI is as important to understand as this one. Once consultants or trainers begin to psychoanalyze their clients, use the MBTI to discuss abilities, predict performance, or in any other way box in, categorize, advantage or disadvantage anyone, they have overstepped their charter. No types are necessarily right and no type is necessarily inappropriate for any job. Too often, while not stated overtly, this is the impression that lingers.

Often, what the MBTI does not measure is almost more important for the audience to understand than what it does measure. Audiences or individual clients often approach the "feedback" session with some trepidation. Frequently, such anxiety stems from having been labeled somewhere by some other "test"—not invariably it was the MMPI, DISC, Personal Profile System, or the FIRO-B that seemed to indicate to them that they were not suited for some aspect of their jobs. My job as a consultant is to understand that their misgivings are not out of the ordinary and to help to set the record straight about the positive, nonrestrictive nature of the MBTI.

Quite simply, the MBTI reports nothing about a client's intelligence, maturity, or possible psychological disturbances. Indeed, as a psychometric tool based on Carl Jung's theory of personality, it has a wellness orientation, not a sickness or pathological orientation. For that reason it has become the most widely selling psychological inventory intended for use with non-psychiatric audiences. Similarly, on a single taking, the MBTI reveals nothing about stress, development, or education. Clients, consequently, need not be apprehensive about taking the MBTI or revealing their results.

What it does measure, is PREFERENCE in four areas of life: how we see reality, how we judge that reality, where we go to get our energy for life, and how others see our orientation to the world. In each of these four areas there are two possible dichotomous choices. The dichotomies are

**Sensing or iNtuition**
**Thinking judgments or Feeling judgments**
**Extraversion or Introversion**
and
**Judging or Perceiving**

Every person has chosen one preference from each pairing as his or her favorite. The combination of the four choices becomes what is called psychological type. In accordance with Jungian theory and its application, as interpreted by Isabel Briggs Myers and her mother, Katharine Briggs, the authors of the MBTI, ties are not permitted; there is, in short, no such thing as an ambivert.

Preferences are transmitted to the client on a report form that shows the number of times a person voted for each preference (these are called raw score points), a set of four letters representing the selected preferences (eg. ESTJ, INFJ, ESFP, or INTP), and a calculated preference strength associated with each selected preference (eg I-23, S-31, T-13, P-9). Usually the preference is plotted on some kind of scale to show the relative clarity of one preference versus the others. The preference strength merely indicates the clarity of the individual's preference. It does not indicate how well developed the particular preference is, nor does it indicate the degree of sophistication with which the person uses that preference. This point is frequently misunderstood by the person receiving the results and even more sadly, by those explaining the results.

Sometimes the words themselves used to identify the eight preferences are also subject to misunderstanding. This section by no means attempts a thorough explanation of the preferences. Such descriptions are plentiful. Isabel Briggs Myers in *Gifts Differing* renders them in their simplest and clearest form. She also offers descriptions of the sixteen types. If there is any criticism at all to be made of her portraits, it is that they are almost too bland—there is not enough definition of nuance. Perhaps the most colorful are found in *Type Talk* by Kroeger and Thuesen— some are a little glib, but the book is designed for the layman. A popularization of type to be sure, *Type Talk* nevertheless attempts to honor both the letter and the spirit of the MBTI heritage and is, in my opinion, the best book currently available to interest the reader in the broad applications of psychological type. Hirsh and Kummerow, likewise, in their fine book *Life Types* describe the preferences singly and in combinations. Their breakout is different from the descriptions available from other authors, preferring to describe the various types in accordance with their, living, learning, laboring, leading, leisure, loving, and losing out styles. Both of these books are highly readable and provide a sound introduction for the novice. *Introduction to Type*, by Isabel Briggs Myers, and *Please Understand Me*, by David Keirsey, also offer substantial descriptions of the preferences.

Where each of these falls short is that they deal with extremes (Myers does the best job at avoiding this problem), and the portraits sometimes become slightly slanted. Keirsey's treatment of types with "N" and "F" preferences, for example, sometimes offends those types. What we get from Kroeger is the extreme of the ENTJ. What we get from Keirsey is the extreme of the ENFP. Hence some readers come away from these books feeling that once again they have been stereotyped. Overall, however, both sets of portraits are superbly rendered.

What is necessary, ideally, is a set of portraits that describe an ESTJ or an INTJ with "good Type Development" (Manual, pp. 14-15). Portraits which might describe an "individuated" type (see Question 23) would likewise be difficult to sketch, but they would go a long way to help diffuse some of the skepticism associated with the pigeonholing that some feel occurs with MBTI literature.

## SENSING OR INTUITION

I prefer to start any description of the preferences with the "S" - "N" difference because it is so easily seen by most audiences and because Jung, himself, although initially seeing extraversion and introversion as the most important distinction, understood the primary forms of mental functioning as perceptions and judgments. According to the theory, we first perceive that which surrounds us and then make judgments, or arrive at closure, about those perceptions. We perceive either by gathering concrete, specific, data (Sensors) or registering concepts, theories, relationships, or possibilities (iNtuitives).

When S's and N's wander through the same office, for example, they both see what is, but what they see is often remarkably different. The sensor may see six desks (four of which are occupied at 10:45 AM), a Remington-500 typewriter, five IBM-200 computer terminals, software scattered across the desks, four clerks (2 male, 2 female) of various races, stacks of white bond paper, three filing cabinets, and a water cooler in need of a replacement bottle. The intuitive, walking through the same office, may report seeing an understaffed, crowded office. Which is real? Which is the correct view of the office? Both, of course, may be equally accurate. Neither is right or wrong, and the more complete description of the office embraces both. But what the sensor has seen is specifics; the intuitive has recorded meanings. Here, then, is the beginning of understanding and appreciating the differences we bring to the workplace.

Sensors are the literalists of the world; the intuitives, more the symbolists and the ones more likely to express their thoughts in metaphor or to see meanings. In other words, does 2 + 2 = 4? Or is 2 + 2 an example of addition? Both are correct ways of interpreting the data. Remember the story about Sylvia and Tracy? Sylvia walks by the corner of Market Street and Fourth Avenue one morning and sees Tracy standing there with a penguin. Rather amazed, she asks, "Tracy, what are you doing with that penguin?" "I don't know," she answered. "It just wandered up and now won't leave. I don't know what to do with it." "Look," said Sylvia. "Why don't you just take it to the Zoo?" "That's a great idea," said Tracy. "I think I will." The next day, Sylvia is walking to work again and passes the same corner. There to her amazement is Tracy again, standing with the same penguin. "I thought you were going to take that penguin to the zoo," said Sylvia. "I did," Tracy replied. "He liked it so much, that today we're going to the theater. " Who is the literalist?

Sometimes this difference can have stark consequences. One of my former students told me a story about his secretary, an ISFP, that helps to underscore this difference. In her previous company, her supervisor had been transferred and a new section chief had taken over. They had offices across the hallway from one another. This section chief had a boss who was suspicious of all new employees who had been transferred from some other part of the organization, and therefore he kept close tabs on them until they proved themselves. For the first week that the new section chief was in the organization, the boss called the ISFP secretary each day about 10:00 am and asked if her boss was "there." Each time he called, the answer was the same: "No sir, I'm sorry, he's not here. Would you like him to call you?" By the fifth day, the boss was livid and finally blurted out: " What time, pray tell, does your new supervisor get into the office?" "Oh," said the ISFP, "about 7:00 am each morning." "Well, why is he never there, then, when I call at 10:00 am," he asked. "Because, sir, his office is across the hall." What, exactly, does **there** mean? Sometimes different things for sensors and intuitives.

It is as though the sensor rips the white paper off from the printer, holds it up and says, "This is reality; this is what we are about in this organization." The intuitive, instead, prefers to report on the possibilities inherent in the data, the relationships between the data, or the decision matrix used to generate the data. Because sensors and intuitives tend to emphasize different aspects of reality, we desperately need each other. Lacking either preference in an organization makes for an environment not nearly as rich in understanding.

One manager from a large chemical firm tells of working with a sister plant in Japan. The manager from the American firm is an intuitive. Virtually the entire leadership of the Japanese plant are sensors. He said it took him a long time to learn how to ask questions of his sensing Japanese counterparts. He originally asked the sensors, "Well, how's the new process going?" The sensors had no idea how to answer his question, which is, by the way, an intuitive phrasing. But, when he asked, "Is the plant working to 85% efficiency in output?", the sensors would respond with, "No, 83%; we expect to be at 85% by October 1st." Intuitives are more comfortable dealing with generalities and approximations. Sensors are more comfortable dealing with specifics and exactness. Each can enrich the other.

What's the point? Why is it so important that we understand this distinction? If you see a fact, but I see a possibility, we can't communicate. Once I realize, however, that both you *and* I have limited views of reality, we can begin to help one another see more clearly. Each is real, but each, alone, is also myopic.

This need we have to understand one another's point of view was recently driven home to me by a friend who tells a story about a trip to Lanzarote in the Canary Islands. She was on an underground tour exploring some caves when the tour guide beckoned everyone to the edge of a deep crevasse. He asked the group to listen carefully as one of the tourists dropped a rock into the crevasse to plumb its depth. What they peered into was an unbelievably deep crevasse that seemed to drop down forever beneath their feet. When the woman dropped the rock, almost immediately there was a splash, and the tourists watched as small ripples quickly spread across the surface of a pond almost at their feet. What they had seen was merely the reflection, on an almost perfectly serene surface, of the cavernous heights above them. The tour guide had had a different perception of reality than they had. But instantly, their perception of reality fell into accord with his. That same flash of recognition rarely occurs for us as we attempt to work with others with greatly different perceptions, but something akin can begin as we come to realize that our view is not the only view of reality.

## THINKING JUDGMENT or FEELING JUDGMENT

Once we have recorded our perceptions, Jung suggests that we have to make some decisions about them. It does not matter how we gathered those perceptions; there is no determining link between our preference for perceiving and our preference for judging. Again, there are two ways of arriving at this closure—both are equally rational, but the rationale that one uses can totally perplex the other. Some people, those called thinking judgers, prefer to evaluate the data rather impersonally—logically assessing the cause and effect relationship among the data. These analytical thinkers tend to objectify the judging process and arrive at closure in a manner that may seem to those with the opposite preference as cool and somewhat insensitive to human concerns.

The others, however, those called feeling judgers, prefer to reason about their perceptions more personally—subjectively reflecting on the effect that their perceptions may have on people, relationships, and interpersonal values. These people can often come across to others, because of their subjectivity, as more concerned, personally involved, and caring than those with the opposite preference. Sometimes this impression is warranted; other times it is not. Some "T"s are very caring; some "F"s are not.

A couple of cautions are in order when addressing the judging function. It is most important to realize that both thinking judgments and feeling judgments are equally rational. Neither has the corner on the market for making quality decisions; they simply reason about their perceptions through different filters. Their mutual rationality, however, is what led Jung to call this pairing the "rational function."

Here's how it might work. Let's say that as the Director of Human Resources you have gotten the assignment to arrange a rather elegant dinner welcoming the new Director of International Marketing for Europe. As a thinking judger—a "T" —you decide to seat people according to a rational method: rank within the organization, job assignment, or position. You might even decide that you will do away with the traditional "pecking order" and simply assign them seats alphabetically. You mention your plan to your deputy, a feeling judger—an "F" —and he or she complains that you have missed the point. Supper is a good time to enhance relationships, so what you should do is to seat people based on who is more compatible with whom or perhaps seat people together who rarely have a chance to speak with one another because they come from diverse geographical locations. Neither approach is more or less correct, but notice the different lenses used to focus the decision.

It is this lens that sometimes brings "T"s and "F"s into conflict. As a "T", I could easily sympathize with the plight of my employees for whom daycare was not just a convenience, but a necessity. My "F" colleague, however, did not sympathize with them, she empathized with them. While I sympathized about their circumstances and wanted to help them find suitable facilities, my F colleague was *there with them*, anguishing with their needs to such an extent that the need became hers as well: EMPATHY, not SYMPATHY.

Recently, working with an INTP plant manager to implement a teambuilding program within his organization, my "F" colleague and I were out-briefing him regarding a series of interviews we had conducted during the day. We had been aware that the day before he had gotten permission from his boss to hire a new technical manager for the plant. He had already decided who the person should be, but had not had time that morning to extend the offer to the person. At the out-briefing, he turned to his director of human resources and said, "I finally got around to offering the job to the person we talked about." As an INTJ, I thought to myself, "hmm, so the NP finally got around to making the offer, and there are just seven days until the person he replaces will be gone. We may have an "NP" leadership problem, here." My "EF" colleague said out loud, "Oh, the poor man. I bet he was dying to find out." In other words, she saw a human relations problem. As a "T," I was concerned with analyzing the process. As an "F," my colleague was concerned with the needs of the person.

What makes the difference? We don't really know. What research has pointed out, however, is that substantially more men are "T"s than "F"s, and substantially more women are "F"s than

"T"s. What this means in the workplace is tremendous pressure on both "F"-men and "T"-women to be more like their genders might suggest. "Shape up or ship out" is an attitude that can have devastating effects on both.

This pair of preferences regarding our judging style is also the one that informs our valuing style. There is, unfortunately, a lot of misunderstanding over this aspect of "T" and "F" among those in the MBTI community. Too many feeling judgers assume that values are their special province. Such is far from the case. Both "F"s and "T"s can be value-centered and each can be value-neutral or worse. Clearly, though, "F"s and "T"s approach valuing differently. "T"s base their values on more objective criteria, "F"s on more subjective criteria. Here's an example that may clarify the difference.

Recently, several employees in a small Virginia consulting firm were discussing some contemporary issues regarding the environment. A few discovered that they shared the same view regarding the debate over tuna fishing. Since thousands of dolphins (the mammal, not the foodfish) are inadvertently killed each year in the process of commercial tuna fishing, these people had all decided to forego eating tuna as a protest against the inhumane drowning of dolphins that occurred when the nets designed for tuna also snared the dolphins who apparently travel together. Three employees, all "F"s, approached management requesting that the firm take a public stance against the tuna industry. The CEO, a "T," agreed, saying she thought the situation morally reprehensible. The "F"s, two men and one woman, were pleasantly surprised by her comments. Only when they began to explore why they had all decided to stop eating tuna did the sparks begin to fly.

As the female CEO explained, "I've decided personally to stop eating tuna because the current practice by many tuna wholesalers encourages the mass destruction of this precious natural resource as a consequence of their current fishing methods. We are in danger of losing a natural resource, without which our planet would be a poorer place." As another "T," I was impressed by her thoughtfulness, zeal, commitment, and sympathetic understanding of the dolphins' plight. The "F"s were appalled!

As they explained it, "Sure, we're in danger of losing a precious, irreplaceable resource, but the real agony is that mammals, just like us, other animals that give birth to live, air-breathing offspring are being viciously smothered under tuna nets just to line fishermen's pockets with more money. It's horrible! I can almost feel myself being dragged down with them, struggling for my last breath, suffocating. God, I feel for them! They are my brothers; they are me. Think of all the stories you have heard of dolphins saving people's lives. How can we stand by and watch them suffer?"

At least in this example, the two sides agreed on the same solution. That's not always the case. But the point is, the MEANS, not the ENDS are what frustrated their organization's harmony — a crucial ingredient for the success of any team.

Consider one more way the "T" - "F" difference can cripple understanding. This incident occurred in July 1990 just after the disastrous earthquake in Iran. After reading in the Washington Post that the earthquake had killed over 40, 000 people, an "F" colleague was talking to her "T" husband about the tragedy. She was trying to express her horror, her sense of loss, her anguish over those who had been killed and injured and the pain she felt for their loved ones. Her "T" husband, attempting to commiserate with her and express his equal concern over the event said warmly, "Try to think of it this way. One day 40,000 people go to a baseball game, but they just don't come back."

See any differences? Don't come back, indeed! The "F" was dumbstruck by what appeared to be the "T"s indifference to human life. The "T" was perplexed, on the other hand, by his wife's inability to see his deep remorse. The "F" prefers to deal with it INSIDE, as part of himself or herself. The "T" deals with it with equal concern, but OUTSIDE of himself or herself. It's not a matter of extraversion or introversion but of attachment or detachment. The "T" has a preference for dealing with such issues in a detached fashion, as though the process took place in a small bubble out in the air, like the bubbles used to indicate dialogue over the heads of cartoon figures. The "F" takes that same bubble and tucks it inside and thinks in terms of I, me, we, you, us. That's the crucial "T" - "F" difference—one that is not easily bridged.

Sadly, we often don't even know when we have offended or perplexed others. Our preferences are so much a part of our personality, so "normal" that the words are out, and feelings bruised before we know it. Some months ago we were sitting in the living room at a friend's house having a friendly chat after dinner. Off to one side of the room was an antique sideboard, the host's (an "F") favorite piece of furniture. One of my associates (a "T") had just returned from working with a team in the Soviet Union. As he described his less than plush accommodations in Moscow, he said, "and the furniture, you can't believe how wretched most of it was. It was just a bunch of uncomfortable old junk, kinda like that thing over there." Yes, he was pointing to the prized heirloom on the other side of the room. As I caught the eyes of another "F" colleague of mine, we could barely keep from bursting out in laughter. If we hadn't been so surprised we probably would have. But the "T" speaking had no idea that he had said anything at all untoward.

## EXTRAVERSION OR INTROVERSION

Once a person's preferences for the modes of perception and judgment are decided, he or she has declared what Jung referred to as the two fundamental forms of mental functioning. The next logical set of differences to explore is what Jung saw early in his career as the most important distinction—that between extraversion and introversion. The difficulty with these words is that they do not necessarily mean to us in general conversation what Jung intended by them in his writings. An extravert is not necessarily loud and talkative, and an introvert is not necessarily shy and withdrawn. But we are stuck with the words because they are Jung's, not ours. Extraverts are those whose interests run to the external world of people and things; introverts are those whose interests run to the internal world of ideas and concepts.

Too often this difference is treated glibly as merely a difference in noise level; the distinction, however, is far richer. I have sat next to introverts on airplane trips who have talked my ear off for the duration of the flight. On the other hand, I have had extraverts seated next to me who spoke only a few sentences throughout the entire flight. The difference is not so neatly drawn between how much is said but rather what is revealed when a person speaks. The introvert may talk incessantly (although, such behavior is not the norm) about President Bush's popularity in the polls, the excitement and challenges inherent in German reunification, the falloff in new starts in the housing markets in the U.S., the turmoil caused by Iraq by annexing Kuwait, or the challenges posed to world trade by the changes destined to occur in Europe in 1992, but the same person will reveal precious little about himself or herself in the process. On the other hand, in just a few succinct phrases (although this is not the norm for extraverts either), my extraverted travel companion would often reveal personal details about himself or herself that would embarrass any self respecting introvert. It is, then, to reiterate, a matter of what we say, not just our volubility, our gregariousness, or our taciturnity.

This difference can often affect how we see others on the same team or in the office. Introverts can mistakenly be seen as poorer "team players" than their extraverted colleagues because they keep so many of the details of their work to themselves. This preference for internal processing often arouses suspicion and distrust among extraverts who prefer to share the details of their work with others. Not infrequently, then, introverts are thought to be operating off of hidden agendas or purposely refusing to keep extraverted colleagues informed of their progress on projects or assignments.

Extraverts, who are much more prone to give freely of information or ideas in their nascent stages than are introverts, may feel threatened or annoyed by their less verbal associates unless they come to understand the introverts' preference for some preliminary innerwork before verbalizing their thoughts—not infrequently, sad to say, after the decision has been made. And, so, the "E" may accuse the "I" of having some kind of hidden agenda.

A not dissimilar frustration occurs for the introvert who is frequently interrupted by extraverts who simply want to update their colleagues on the current status of their thinking. "Thank-you for sharing," thinks the introvert, "but who cares?"

In an environment that encourages the sharing of information—particularly the data-rich world of modern business—or professions where "networking" is the name of game, the introvert can become truly disadvantaged. In meetings where brainstorming is the modus operandi, the introvert may feel ill-at-ease. Worse yet, the introvert may be perceived as a poor team player because he or she has not taken an active role in the generation of ideas, options, data, or approaches. At worst they may be seen as disruptive of the process established by the team leader. The extraverts tend to shape the discussion, run the meetings, overpower the brainstorming process, and often get involved in verbal blood-letting in an effort to get their fair share of air-time. Introverts often enter the fray after they have thought through similar issues inside, but then they appear to be arriving just in time to pillage the battlefield and pick up the pieces. Actually, both introverts and extraverts are merely working in that world (INNER or OUTER) that they find to be most preferred. Neither is attempting to undermine or to overpower the other, but without the knowledge the MBTI can provide, we frequently misread others' motives.

Each can disadvantage the other on the staff unless their particular needs can be understood and accommodated. The Introvert must respect the extravert's need for frequent feedback and not be so quick to act on each thought the extravert advances—the thought may be, after all, just in outline form. The "E" may not have thought through the idea at all, but the "I" assumes that activity has already taken place. Equally necessary is the extravert's respect for the introvert's preference for quieter, more solitary work. One simple way to help tap the talents of the introverted staff member in meetings where otherwise he or she may be less prone to take an active role, is to publish the agenda in advance or to keep an open agenda posted for a few days prior to the meeting. This technique gives the introvert an opportunity to do the preferred internal pre-work before the meeting and may even enrich the extraverts' contributions by enabling them to talk through some of their thoughts before commenting publicly in the meeting.

Our experience is that this attitude is often the most disruptive dimension in relationships both in the office and at home. Extraverts, once they really appreciate the introverts' strength, can begin to realize that not all introverts are plotting behind their backs. Concomitantly, introverts, once they recognize the extraverts' strength, can begin to understand the extraverts' need to talk through issues, ideas, and decisions. Each has much to learn from the other.

One other aspect that extraverts and introverts differ on in clear ways is in their attitudes toward comfort in their settings, what is often called spatiality. I remember watching a briefing in the Pentagon recently where a male lieutenant colonel was briefing a female colonel. He walked into the briefing room, marched right up to her table, and in a truly extraverted way began to brief her on a project, standing about two feet in front of her. She let him get about five or six sentences into his presentation and said, "Hold it! Are you here to brief me or make love to me?" In other words, this introvert was saying, you have invaded my personal space—back off! He took about three steps to the rear, apologized, and to his credit continued his pitch without missing a beat. The difference, however, is one of spatiality—what's yours and what's mine.

To their credit, educators are becoming more and more aware of another aspect of this difference in the classroom. Introverts, who are quite spatial compared with extraverts, can be disadvantaged in the classroom by teachers who change students' seating assignments several times during the semester. Just when the introverts get comfortable with their space, they are moved to a new spot. Where this phenomenon of spatiality is particularly noticeable is when the introverted child has to change schools or just move to a new classroom at the beginning of the school year. A parent can save a lot of transition time for an introverted child by merely taking that child to the classroom where he or she will spend the next semester and letting the child sit in his or her seat for a few minutes before the rest of the children arrive—the day before or the week before school starts. That way, when introverted Ainsley has to stand up Monday morning and introduce herself to the rest of the class, she is welcoming them to HER class.; she's not the new kid in their classroom. But while we are getting better recognizing this dilemma in the classroom, we are still slow at dealing with it in the business world.

Too many people—even those claiming to be skilled users of the MBTI—still merely give lip service to such diversity in the workplace. When it comes to honoring it, they fall far short of the mark. One business colleague and I had a major falling out over the issue of my spatiality. My "E" colleague would occasionally finish a day's training at 5:00 pm, that evening hop a flight to another city, arrive at 8:00 or 9:00 pm, catch a limo to the hotel, check in about 10:30 or 11:00 pm, and be prepared to train again the next day at 8:00 am. He would breeze in at 7:45 and be ready to go. I could do, and frequently did, the same thing. However, my preference would be to make myself comfortable with my new space first. That way I could guarantee my best work. I needed to arrive early and become comfortable with the new surroundings. To do that, I preferred arriving the evening before and running five to ten miles in the new environment. As a marathoner, I just enjoy running, but more importantly, as an introvert, once I have run the streets in a city, I feel at home there—it's my town, my space.

On one occasion, I was co-training with a competent partner for a full week. Previously, I had also been booked by my employer for an all-day presentation in another city in the middle of that week. The plan was for my co-trainer to take over for me while I was gone on Wednesday and teach the entire day by herself. The day I was scheduled to leave, I taught the entire morning session and after lunch until 3:00 pm. At that time I left to catch a flight at 6:00 pm which would put me in the next city by 7:00 pm, in the hotel by 9:00 pm, and on the streets running by 9:15 pm. The next day I arrived at the training site by 7:00 am to prepare for a major training event with a new client scheduled to begin at 8:00 am. At 8:00 am the audience arrived and entered MY AUDITORIUM—spatiality. My "E" employer docked me a half day's pay for the day I left two hours early in order to fulfill a contract she had scheduled, claiming I probably had some "hidden agenda" for wanting to do things differently from my ultra-extraverted colleague. That misunderstanding was caused entirely by our differences regarding spatiality. The MBTI has been available to consultants since 1975, but we still have a lot of educating to do, even among our own ranks.

Let me suggest one more aspect of Extraversion which is often missed. As I was writing this text, a friend called to tell me her experiences with several audiences with which she had recently been working. As an ENTJ, she was surprised to find that after a workshop she had a difficult time disengaging herself from the group. She thought "T"s could do that with some ease. She wanted to pursue their discussions, help them to grow even more, and after she had left felt somehow empty because their contact had ceased. The issue is one the extravert often faces. Not only does the extravert get empowered by others, but their sense of connectedness is often greater than the introvert's. Once the engagement has ended the extravert often experiences a bewildering sense of loss or continued "high."

## JUDGING OR PERCEIVING

This last choice is quick to breed ill will and disharmony in organizations. The choice is between the preference to order and structure experiences or the preference to ride with the tide, go with the flow, or simply to react to experiences. The person with a judging preference—a "J"—has a passion for ORGANIZA-TION, whereas the person with a perceiving preference—a "P"— has a passion for ADAPTABILITY. This often is the easiest preference to identify because we have such unflattering labels for those who do not share our attitudes. Neither the "P" nor the "J," without training, is likely to appreciate the other's attitude toward closure or spontaneity.

"P"s tend to exasperate "J"s with their seemingly bottomless supply of new suggestions or alternative ways of accomplishing a project. In fact it is not unusual for "J"s simply to decide that the "P"'s last alternative is the decision and to implement it accordingly. Contrariwise, "J"s can perplex"P"s with their passion for order, structure, and closure. But the "P," expecting just a little more data, often seems to ignore the closure the "J" intended, and the decision goes unheeded. This kind of static in communication breeds dysfunctional behavior.

How many times have you been in a meeting and observed something like this? Just when the "J" thinks all the options have been tabled and the data can be weighed to arrive at a decision, the "P" plunks down just one more consideration that ought to be included in the equation. The "P" probably thought the "J" was moving too swiftly to closure and wanted to forestall a poor decision. The problem, from the "P"'s perspective, is that "J"s sound certain; they come across as seeming to know the right answer (sometimes, even without the necessary data). As I used to tell members of a negotiating team with whom I was working (a team composed predominantly of "J"s), "It's tough to teach negotiating skills to people who know they are right." Unfortunately, that attitude is sometimes a "J" problem. "P"s need to keep in mind, however, that "J"s are not always as sure of themselves as they sound. On the other hand, "J"s must be part of the decision-making process or the team may get around to deciding far too slowly. But the "J"s must give the "P"s the opportunity to surface their ideas. Both judgers and perceivers, therefore, are necessary for a smoothly functioning team. Neither is right and neither is wrong.

In the competitive business world of the 1990's we cannot afford to miss the richness that an understanding of type can add to our relationships. It has been quipped that **foresight** is better than **hindsight**, but **insight** is the best of all. Well, the MBTI provides us just those **insights** into our preferred styles of perceiving reality, of making judgments regarding those perceptions, of where we do our best work, and how others see us in regard to our relative openness or closedness. In short, it provides us with the most effective tool available for understanding communications and relationships between people. In an increasingly complex world where not only are we having to do more with less, but do it better, faster, and more stylishly, and at the same time move with greater ease across cultural and international boundaries, psychological type offers an unmatchable resource. It is the very corporate leverage every forward-looking firm needs in order to do the quality team building crucial for success in the exciting years ahead.

# Selected Bibliography

Some of the following works are cited in the answers to the questions. All, however, should be in the library of any serious student of type.

Barr, Lee, and Norma Barr. *The Leadership Equation*. Austin TX: Eakin Press, 1989.

Bates, Marilyn, and David Keirsey. *Please Understand Me*. DelMar, CA: Prometheus Book Company, 1978.

Bennet, E. A. *What Jung Really Said*. New York: Schocken Books, 1983.

*Bibliography: The Myers-Briggs Type Indicator*. Gainesville,FL: Center for Applications of Psychological Type, continually updated listing.

Brownsword, Alan. *It Takes All Types*. Baytree Publication Company.

Campbell, Joseph, ed. *The Portable Jung*. New York: Viking Press, 1971.

Gilligan, Carol. *In A Different Voice*. Cambridge, MA: Harvard University Press, 1982.

Hall, Calvin S. and Vernon Nordby. *A Primer of Jungian Psychology*. New York: Viking Books, 1973.

Hirsh, Sandra Krebs. *Using the Myers-Briggs Type Indicator In Organizations*. Palo Alto, CA: Consulting Psychologists Press, 1985.

Hirsh, Sandra Krebs, and Jean M. Kummerow. *Introduction to Type In Organizations*. Palo Alto, CA: Consulting Psychologists Press, 1987, rev. 1990.

Hirsh, Sandra Krebs, and Jean Kummerow. *LIFETypes*. New York: Warner Books, 1989.

Isachsen, Olaf, and Linda V. Berens. *Working Together*. Coronado, CA: NEWORLD MANAGEMENT PRESS, 1988.

Johnson, Robert A. *Innerwork*. San Francisco, CA: Harper & Row, 1989.

Jung, C. G. *Memories, Dreams, Reflections*.ed. A. Jaffe, New York: Harcourt & Brace, 1923.

Jung, C. G. *Psychological Types*. Trans. by H. G. Baynes, Rev. by R. F. C. Hull. Princeton: Princeton University Press, 1974.

Kroeger, Otto, and Janet M. Thuesen. *Type Talk*. New York: Delacorte Press, 1988.

Lawrence, Gordon. *People Types and Tiger Stripes*. 2nd ed. Gainesville, FL: Center for Applications of Psychological Type, 1982.

McCaulley, Mary H. *Introduction to the MBTI for Researchers*. Gainesville, FL: Center for Applications of Psychological Type, 1977.

McCaulley, Mary H. *Jung's Theory of Psychological Types and the Myers-Briggs Type Indicator*. Gainesville, FL: Center for Applications of Psychological Type, 1981.

Macdaid, Gerald P., Mary H. McCaulley, and Richard I. Kainz. *Myers-Briggs Type Indicator Atlas of Type Tables*. Gainesville, FL: Center for Applications of Psychological Type, 1986.

Myers, Isabel Briggs. *Gifts Differing*. Palo Alto, CA: Consulting Psychologists Press, 1980.

Myers, Isabel Briggs. *Introduction To Type*. Rev. ed. Palo Alto, CA: Consulting Psychologists Press, 1987.

Myers, Isabel Briggs. *Type and Teamwork*. Gainesville, FL: Center for Applications of Psychological Type, 1974.

Myers, Isabel Briggs, and Mary H. McCaulley. *Manual: A Guide to the Development and the Use of the Myers-Briggs Type Indicator*. Palo Alto, CA: Consulting Psychologists Press, 1985.

Page, Earle C. *Looking at Type*. Gainesville, FL: Center for Applications of Psychological Type, 1987.

Schemel, George J., and James A. Borbely. *Facing Your Type*. Wernersville, PA: Typrofile Press, 1982.

von Franz, Marie-Louise, and James Hillman. *Lectures on Jung's Typology*. Irving TX: Spring Publications, 1971.

# ABOUT THE AUTHOR

William Jeffries is an organizational development consultant specializing in creative applications of the Myers-Briggs Type Indicator. He has been a soldier, scholar, manager, and educational administrator. He is a recognized expert in the field of professional ethics and a gifted speaker on the subject of human resource development. In addition to having taught at the undergraduate and graduate levels, he has, during the past 10 years, consulted for industry, public and private schools, universities, corporations, government agencies, church groups, small businesses, and the armed forces. His undergraduate studies at West Point focused on engineering and industrial management and his graduate studies at Duke University were in language, literature, and values. During his 20 years in the military, he served in Europe, South East Asia, and the United States as a commander, advisor, staff officer, and educator. As a tenured Associate Professor in the Department of English at West Point, he directed courses of study in Comparative World Literature and Freshman Composition and taught a variety of interdisciplinary elective courses relating literature to contemporary culture, psychology, religion, and values. While teaching Philosophy and Ethics, he edited "Ethics and the MIlitary Profession." As a faculty member of the Armed Forces Staff College, National Defense University, he created a course of study entitled The Foundations of Moral Enquiry based on an original model of ethical decision-making and served as the Director of Executive Development for the college, where he created a program of study stressing a holistic approach to psychological, physical, managerial, ethical, and intellectual development for mid-career, military officers and civilian government executives. He is also an adjunct faculty member of Old Dominion University where he teaches a graduate course entitled Ethics and Law in Higher Education.

He has written essays on values, the Myers-Briggs Type Indicator, Russian Literature, human ethnology, religion, and mythology and has published monographs on "War and Morality," "The Professional Ethic," and "Can Ethics Be Taught?" His "Organizational Survey" is widely used to assess the success of interventions in organizations, and he has also edited a Career Assessment Workbook and a Personal Goals Workbook. His current writing is on team building, ethics, and problem solving in organizations.

Bill is affiliated with several scholarly and professional organizations including The Honor Society of Phi Kappa Phi, The Association of Psychological Type, the Joint Services Conference on Professional Ethics, The Association for Supervision and Curriculum Development, the National Council of Teachers of English, The American Chamber of Commerce in Belgium, and Rotary International.

Over the last several years, Bill has participated in numerous programs designed to enhance Leadership in a World Environment: "Leadership Development Program" Hoechst Celanese Corporation

"Leadership for a Democratic Society" The Federal Executive Institute

"Program for Executives" Carnegie Mellon University

"Expert Teachers Academy" Virginia Association of Independent Schools

"Senior Federal Executive Program" U. S. Department of Health and Human Services

"Typewatching Qualifying Workshop" and "Corporate Dynamics" Otto Kroeger Associates

"Executive Development Program" National Defense University

"Basics of Supervisory Skills"  U. S. Department of Agriculture "Managing for Results"  Environmental Protection Agency
"Executive Management Development Program"  USDA Food Safety Inspectors
"Creativity in the Workplace" Dupont Corporation
"City of Richmond Management Academy"
"West Virginia State Teachers Academy"
"Leadership for the 90's"  Rhone-Poulenc

He is currently president of **Executive Strategies International,** where he has brought together a diverse group of consulting associates specializing in organizational and human behavior to meet the organizational development needs of the international community of the 1990's. Typical Workshops Include:

* Work Design
* Introduction to the MBTI
* Organizational Uses of the MBTI
* Career Transitions
* Ethics
* Team-Building
* Creative Problem Solving
* Using the Murphy-Meisgeier Type Indicator for Children
* Cross-Cultural Applications of Training
* Teaching and Learning Styles
* Futuring and Strategic Planning
* Understanding Relationships in the 1990's
* Organizational Assessments

Would you like to be notified as we publish new books in your area of interest? Would you like a copy of our latest catalog? If so, fill in the address form (or copy it, if you prefer to leave this book uncut), and send to:

Hampton Roads Publishing Company, Inc.
891 Norfolk Square
Norfolk, VA 23502

[ ] Please send latest catalog

[ ] Please add me to the mailing list

NAME: _____

ADDRESS: _____

CITY: _____

STATE: _____ ZIP: _____